Routledge Revivals

Towards International Government

First published in 1915, *Towards International Government* considers the consequences of war for global diplomacy and the alliance system. Hobson argues that, to reduce armaments and the possibility of another world war, an organisational structure of international government must be put into place. An extension of the League of Nations, Hobson proposes that this council would need to hold legislative powers enabling it to impose economic sanctions and, if necessary, the ability to deploy an international force. This is a fascinating and exceptionally forward-thinking work, of great importance to economic and political historians of the twentieth century.

Towards International Government

J. A. Hobson

Routledge
Taylor & Francis Group
Routledge Revivals

First published in 1915
by George Allen & Unwin Ltd

This edition first published in 2013 by Routledge
2 Park Square, Milton Park, Abingdon, Oxon, OX14 4RN

Simultaneously published in the USA and Canada
by Routledge
711 Third Avenue, New York, NY 10017

Routledge is an imprint of the Taylor & Francis Group, an informa business

Publisher's Note
The publisher has gone to great lengths to ensure the quality of this reprint but points out that some imperfections in the original copies may be apparent.

Disclaimer
The publisher has made every effort to trace copyright holders and welcomes correspondence from those they have been unable to contact.

A Library of Congress record exists under LC control no: 16001033

ISBN 13: 978-0-415-82075-2 (hbk)
ISBN 13: 978-0-203-55201-8 (ebk)

Towards International Government

BY

J. A. HOBSON

AUTHOR OF "WORK AND WEALTH: A HUMAN VALUATION," "IMPERIALISM," ETC.

LONDON: GEORGE ALLEN & UNWIN LTD.
RUSKIN HOUSE 40 MUSEUM STREET, W.C.

First published in 1915

PREFACE

AFTER this war is over, will the nations fall back again into the armed peace, the rival alliances, the Balance of Power with competing armaments, the preparations for another war thus made "inevitable," or will they go forward to the realization of the idea of "public right," as expounded by Mr. Asquith, "the substitution for force, for the clash of competing ambitions, for groupings and alliances and a precarious equipoise, of a real European partnership, based on the recognition of equal rights and established and enforced by the common will"?[1] The preservation and progress of civilization demand that the peoples go forward. But how shall "public right" be realized?

The issue is, perhaps, best approached by putting a narrower, more concrete question: How can nations be got to reduce their armaments? For this action will be the best test and pledge of the establishment of "public right" and the reliance on a pacific future. Could a conference of Powers bring about a reduction of armaments by agreement? Surely not unless the motives which have led them in the past to arm are reversed. These motives are either a desire to be stronger than

[1] Dublin, September 25th, 1914.

some other Power, in order to take something from him by force—the aggressive motive ; or a desire to be strong enough to prevent some other Power from acting in this way to us—the defensive motive. Now how can these motives be reversed? Nations may enter into a solemn undertaking to refer all differences or disputes that may arise to arbitration or to other peaceful settlement. If they can be got to adhere to such a general agreement, international law and public right will take the place of private force, and wars of aggression and defence will no longer happen. But what will ensure the fulfilment of their undertaking by all the signatory Powers? Public opinion and a common sense of justice are found inadequate safeguards. There must be an executive power enabled to apply an economic boycott, or in the last resort an international force. If this power is adequate, it will secure the desired reversal of the offensive and the defensive motives to armaments, and will by a natural process lead to a reduction of national forces.

But it is not safe for the League of Nations to wait until difficulties ripen into quarrels. There must be some wider power of inquiry and settlement vested in a representative Council of the Nations. This will in substance mean a legislative power. For peace cannot be secured by adopting a purely statical view of the needs and rights of nations in relation to one another. New applications of the principles of political " autonomy " and of " the open door " will become necessary, and some international method of dealing with them is essential. So there emerges the necessity of extending the idea of a League of Peace into that of an International Government.

Such is the general argument of these chapters, highly speculative in parts, but directed to the needs of the situation. Many difficulties come up for consideration. What nations would enter into such an international arrangement, and upon what terms of representation? Should it be a European Confederation, or is a wider basis wanted? Finally, the reader is confronted with the objections of political theorists and historians, to the effect that all these ambitious designs are Utopian. But these objections do not take account of the new factors in the modern situation, and in particular of the rising consciousness of power in the Peoples. The new era of internationalism requires the replacement of the secret diplomacy of Powers by the public intercourse of Peoples through their chosen representatives. If the Peace which ends this war is to be durable, it must be of a kind to facilitate the setting-up of these new international arrangements. No timid, tentative quarter measures will suffice. Courage and faith are needed for a great new extension of the art of government.

The writer is well aware that his proposals and the argument by which he recommends them form an outlined sketch rather than a scheme of internationalism. Countless practical difficulties are no doubt thus evaded which will need close discussion before any substantial progress along these lines can be realized. But it seemed desirable that some such rapid and hazardous advance of speculative thought should be made, even though it might be found that some of the positions could not be " held " while others had to be " reconstituted." Even had he felt qualified to set forth his proposals in closer-worked designs, he would have refrained from doing so. For at the present stage it is of paramount importance to try to get the largest number of thoughtful people to form clear, general ideas of better international relations, and to desire their attainment. To bury these new-formed ideas beneath mountains of detail, however relevant, is for the time a bad intellectual and moral economy. It may, indeed, be the case that this mode of appeal ignores or extenuates some difficulties and dangers that are deep-rooted in the nature of man or of national life, and are not of mere detail. The writer has had an interesting experience of these deeper differences of opinion and judgment as a member of a Committee which, under the guidance of Lord Bryce, has met constantly during the course of the war for the consideration of a constructive policy in international relations. To his fellow-members on this Committee he owes much in the way of information and of suggestion, and to two in particular, Mr. G. Lowes Dickinson and Mr. E. R. Cross, he wishes to express a special sense of obligation for the service they have rendered him in reading the manuscript of this work and in offering valued criticism of its contents.

HAMPSTEAD,
July 1915.

CONTENTS

TOWARDS INTERNATIONAL GOVERNMENT

CHAPTER I

A LEAGUE OF PEACE

ALMOST everybody hopes that, when this war is over, it will be possible to secure the conditions of a lasting peace by reducing the power of militarism and by setting the relations between nations on a better footing. To watchers of the present conflict it seems an intolerable thought that, after the fighting is done, we should once more return to a condition of "armed peace," with jealous, distrustful, and revengeful Powers piling up armaments and plotting singly or in groups against their neighbours until Europe is plunged into another war more terrible, more bloody, and more costly than this. Yet nothing is more certain than that this will happen unless the Peoples which are so vitally concerned are able to mobilize their powers of clear thought, sane feeling, and goodwill in carefully considered plans for a co-operative policy of nations.

The first great obstacle to the performance of

this task is the state of mind of those who seem to think that all that is required is "to crush German militarism," and that, this incubus once removed, the naturally pacific disposition of all other nations will dispose them to live together in amity. It is not easy to induce such persons to consider closely what they mean by "crushing German militarism," or how its destruction, whatever it does mean, would secure the peace of Europe, we will not say in perpetuity, but for a single generation. But let us suppose the most complete success for the arms of the Allies, the slaughter or the capture of great German forces, the invasion of Germany, and the dictation of terms of peace by the Allies at Berlin. Such terms as were imposed might cripple her military power of aggression or revenge for some years. But would it kill what we know as German militarism? If our accepted political analysis be right, the German militarism that must be crushed is not an army and a navy, but a spirit of national aggression, proud, brutal, and unscrupulous, the outcome of certain intellectual and moral tendencies embodied in the "real" politics and the "real" culture of the nation. Can we seriously suppose that this evil spirit will be exorcised by a crushing defeat on land and sea, followed by a humiliating peace? If Germany could be permanently disabled from entertaining any hopes of recovering her military strength, or from exercising any considerable influence in the high policy of Europe, her feelings of resentment and humiliation might perhaps be left to rankle in impotence, or to die out by lapse of time. But nothing which the Allies can do to Germany will leave her in such long-lasting impotence. Even if stripped of her non-Teutonic lands and populations, she will remain a great Power—great in area, population, industry, and organizing power—and no temporary restrictions or guarantees can long prevent her from once more developing a military strength that will give dangerous meaning to her thirst for vengeance. Whether the hegemony of Prussia over a confederation of German States (possibly including Austria) be retained or not, Europe can have no security that the same passions which stirred France to the most strenuous efforts to recover her military strength after 1870 will not be similarly operative throughout Germany. We cannot feel sure that the experience of the most disastrous war will effectively destroy the hold of Prussianism, and that the efficiency of intellect and will which constitute that power will not be able to re-assert their sway over a broken Germany.

The fear of such a revival of German strength will remain ever-present in her neighbours, and will compel them to maintain great military preparations. A beaten Germany, with a ring of military Powers round her, watching every phase of her recovery with suspicion, and always liable to quarrel among themselves, will not give peace to Europe. Even, therefore, if we assign to Germany a monopoly of the spirit of aggressive militarism, European peace is not secured by crushing Germany. A saner review of the situation, however, will recognize that Germany has no such monopoly of the spirit of aggression, though that spirit has in her recent policy found its most formidable and most conscious expression. If the craving for a colonial Empire with "places in the sun" was, as seems likely, the principal factor in the aggressive designs of Germany, can we confidently assert that no other State has in the past harboured such designs, or may not harbour them again? The expansive Imperialism of Great Britain, France, Russia, and even more recently of Japan, gives the lie to any such assertion. Pan-Slavism is in spirit identical with the Pan-Teutonism which has contributed to this *débâcle*, and Great Britain and France are already sated with the overseas Empire which Germany was craving. History shows that, in every militarist State, aggressive and defensive motives and purposes are present together in different degrees at all times. While, therefore, we may reasonably think that the aggressive militarism of Germany held increasing sway in the political direction of that Empire during recent years, and was the direct efficient cause of the present conflict, we cannot hold that, with the defeat or even the destruction of the military and naval power of Germany, militarism would tend to disappear from the European system, and that the relations between nations would henceforth undergo so radical a change as to secure the world against all likelihood of forcible outbreaks in the future.

Clearly, it is not German militarism alone, but militarism in general that must be broken. The real question is how to change the inner attitude of nations, their beliefs and feelings towards one another, so as to make each nation and its rulers recognize that it is no longer either desirable or feasible to seek peculiar advantages for itself by bringing force to bear upon another nation.

But it may be urged, granted that disarmament may not be set afoot spontaneously and separately by the different nations, mutual disarmament can occur by arrangement between the Powers, which, after the menace of German aggression is removed, will be disposed to take this step in concert. Such disarmament, it is usually conceived, will not stand alone, but will form an important feature of a larger international policy, by which the Powers will agree among themselves to settle any differences that may arise by reference to courts of conciliation or of arbitration, and perhaps also to concert measures of common action in dealing with States and territories not within their jurisdiction. Such a concert of European Powers has hitherto appeared to many to yield an adequate basis for the peace of Europe, if it could be brought about. It has also seemed to most men the utmost limit of the actually attainable. The idea of the possibility of any closer relation between sovereign independent States has been dismissed as chimerical.

Now in any discussion of the feasibility of such a concert of European or world Powers as will by mutual agreement secure disarmament and a settlement of differences by judicial methods, it must be recognized at the outset that this war may make the successful pursuance of such a policy more difficult than it would have been before. A Balance of Power, whatever may have been its other disadvantages, seemed in itself favourable to the possibilities of an agreement in which each nation, or group of nations, might be an equal gainer. But a decisive victory in war, which leaves the Allied nations with a strong preponderance of power, is less likely to yield a satisfactory basis of agreement for a mutual disarmament. Is it likely that they will readily consent to a reduction in their several military and naval forces equivalent to the reduction they will demand in the forces of the nations that have been their enemies? To put the difficulty in concrete terms: Would France consent to an early reduction of her army upon terms which would leave her fighting-strength as compared with that of Germany relatively the same as before the war? Would Great Britain consent to reduce her navy in the same proportion as the reduction she required of Germany? Even if the Allies believed that the proportionate reduction would be duly carried out by Germany, would they regard such an arrangement as affording the desired security? Obviously not. It may, of course, be urged that an agreed basis of reduction might be reached, according to which the relative strength of army and navy assigned to Germany would be smaller than before. But the more closely the proposition is examined the less feasible does it appear. What basis for the size of armies could reasonably, or even plausibly, be suggested which would not assign to Germany a larger preponderance over France in number of soldiers than she possesses at present? Size of population, or of frontiers, the two most reasonable considerations for apportioning defensive needs, would tell in favour of Germany against France. True it would tell even more strongly in favour of Russia, assigning her, in fact, a relatively larger military predominance in Europe than she has ever claimed. But would either France or Germany regard the new military situation as safe or desirable? Nor would there be any permanence in an arrangement based on such a mutable factor as population, according to which the German preponderance over France and of Russia over Germany would be continually increasing. If area of territory, as well as population and frontiers, were taken into consideration in fixing a basis, France would come off a little better in relation to Germany, but the size of Russia, even if her European lands were alone included, would give her an overwhelming advantage. If, as might not unreasonably be claimed, the extra-European possessions of Russia, Great Britain, and France must be reckoned in, either on a basis of territory or of population, Great Britain and Russia would possess a superiority of military strength which would give them, acting together, a complete control over the politics of Europe and Asia. Or, were the United States to come into the arrangement, the military strength of Anglo-Saxondom might too obviously surpass that of any likely combination of other Powers.

Again, what basis of naval strength would be satisfactory? Great Britain would not think of accepting the area, population, or frontier factors unless the Empire as well as the British Isles were counted in. On the other hand, her proposal, that volume of shipping and of foreign trade should count heavily in the basis, might give her for the time being an even greater preponderance over other navies than she has hitherto possessed.

If the comparison of the military and naval strength of nations were conducted, as in the past, by direct consideration of the numerical strength and the fighting value of the several items of an army and a navy, agreement upon a basis of reduction would be manifestly impossible. The discovery and acceptance of any standard unit of naval or military value applicable to changing conditions of modern warfare are found to be impracticable. For though every military budget implies the acceptance of some scale of values by which the worth of a battery of artillery is compared with that of a battalion of infantry, while every naval budget involves a calculation of the worth of a submarine or a seaplane as compared with an armoured cruiser and a super-Dreadnought, no two budgets would be found to support the same scale of values. It is quite manifest that no agreement for reducing armaments could be attained by stipulations as to the number, size, or quality of the several forces and arms employed. This difficulty in itself, however, is not fatal to the proposal. For a far simpler and more satisfactory method of agreement might be found by disregarding the concrete armaments and accepting a financial basis of expenditure which would leave each nation complete liberty to apply the money prescribed to it as a maximum expenditure on armaments in whatever way it chose. Though each nation, considering its defence, would doubtless have to take into account the sort of preparations for possible attack its neighbours might be making, it would be entitled to spend as large a proportion of its authorized expenditure upon guns, torpedo-boats, aircraft, Dreadnoughts, as it chose.

The real difficulty, therefore, turns upon the agreement upon a basis of comparative expenditure. Now this difficulty appears insuperable, if reduction of armaments be regarded as the sole, or the chief, mainstay of a durable peace. For so long as the motives which have hitherto impelled nations to increase their armaments still retain the appearance of validity in any nation or group of nations, no agreed basis for reduction will be reached, or, were it reached, no reliable adherence to its terms could be expected. For the reduction of armaments involves the acceptance of and the adherence to a principle of reduction by all the Great Powers. If any single Great Power refused to come into the agreement, or, coming in, was suspected of evading the fulfilment of its pledge by concealing some of its expenditure on armaments, this method would have failed *pro tanto*, both as an economy and a security. For each of the would-be pacific nations would have to make adequate provision against the warlike outsider or suspect. Now, that a mere agreement for mutual disarmament would thus be baffled is almost certain. So long as a Power, by simply refusing to come in, could retain full liberty to pile up arms with a view to a future policy of menace or aggression, would there not be Governments which would find some more or less plausible excuses for declining the invitation to come in? Or could we feel complete assurance that a Power with an aggressive past, after entering into such an agreement, would faithfully fulfil it when so many facilities of evasion present themselves? Nay, there would be a positive incentive to an aggressive or revengeful Power either to stay outside, or, entering in, to violate secretly its obligations. For, by either course, it would be enabled to steal a march in military strength over its intended enemy, if the latter were a faithful adherent to such a treaty. The slightest reflection suffices to show that a mere agreement for disarmament or reduction of armament must be futile.

But, it will be contended, these difficulties may be overcome by extending the agreement so as to bind the signatory Powers to bring their united force to bear upon any member convicted of a wilful evasion or infraction of the agreement. That is to say, they must engage to secure the agreement by an ultimate sanction of physical force. The administration of such an agreement would, of course, involve the setting up of some standing Court or Committee of Inquiry, vested with full rights of inspection and judgment, and endowed with a power of armed executive.

But if a treaty of reduction of armaments could be secured by such a guarantee of collective force, it would still find itself confronted by the problem of the lawless outsider. So long as an aggressive outsider were at liberty to threaten or coerce a member of the League without involving the hostility of the other members, this danger would compel members of the League to maintain large armaments, though they were secure against internal hostility. A single Power, such as Germany, Russia, or Japan, standing out for its absolute right to determine its own expenditure and policy, would cancel nearly all the economy of the agreement. It would become self-evident that the Powers entering such an agreement must bind themselves to a common defence against such an outsider. They would be impelled to this course by a double motive. In no other way could each member gain that security which would win his consent to a basis of reduction that would lower his separate defensive power. Again, by pledging themselves to united action against an aggressive outside Power, they would diminish, perhaps destroy, the aggressive design or policy of such a Power. For such aggressive policy and the armed force which supports it are only plausible upon the assumption that they can be successfully applied to gain a selfish national end. If the united strength of the Treaty Powers remained so great as to render the pursuance of its aggressive designs impossible or too dangerous, the lawless Power might learn the lesson of the law, and, abandoning its hopes of aggression, come into the League.

In a word, the proposal for reduction of armaments only becomes really feasible when it is linked with a provision for reversing the *motives* which lead nations to increase their armed forces. Once bring to bear upon the Governments of States a clear recognition of the two related facts : first, that by no increase of their armed force will they be reasonably likely to succeed in any aggressive design upon a neighbour ; second, that by the pledged co-operation of their cosignatories they are not dependent for defence upon their own force alone, then obvious motives of economy and self-interest will lead them to reduce their armaments. Though the military caste may still plead the instability of pacific agreements and the disciplinary advantages of National Service, while contractors for armaments do their best to sow dissension among the leagued Powers and to arouse the military ambitions of new nations, these war interests would no longer be able to play as heretofore upon the fears and passions of the peoples. For whatever the secret political and business policy behind the race for armaments, its engineers could only make that policy effective by periodic appeals to the menace of invasion. Once make it manifest that no evil-minded foreigner can threaten aggression against one country without meeting an overwhelming strength of leagued forces, to which one particular contribution is not of determinant importance, and the balance of national motives leans heavily and constantly towards smaller and less expensive forces.

The absolute strength of the rational and moral case against war and militarism has in some degree obscured the fact that, so long as pushful statesmen and diplomatists, ambitious soldiers, covetous financiers, and war-traders were able to stimulate and carry out aggressive policies of conquest and aggrandizement on the part of stronger against weaker States, the apprehensions upon which these same interests played in urging the necessity of large expenditure upon defence were not unreasonable. It is only by making it too obviously difficult and dangerous for any one Power to attack any other Power that the balance of reasonable motives is firmly weighted against armaments. This can only be achieved by substituting for a world of isolated independent States, or of Balances of Power, a world in which the united strength of a sufficient number of States is brought to bear immediately and certainly against any disturber of the public peace.

"Splendid isolation" is no longer practicable in the modern world of international relations. Group alliances in pursuit of the Balance of Power are seen to be nothing else than an idle feint. For the sole and constant aim of each such group and Power is not to achieve or to maintain the balance, but to weight it on one side. Such an alternating and oscillating balance gives the maximum of insecurity, and thus plays most effectively the game of war and armaments. The only possible alternative is the creation of such a concert or confederation of Powers as shall afford to each the best available security against the aggression of another within the concert and the best defence of all against aggression from outside.

CHAPTER II

A BASIS OF CONFEDERATION

THE general form in which a co-operation of nations for these objects presents itself is that of a League or Confederation. The primary object of such a League is to bind all its members to submit all their serious differences to arbitration or some other mode of peaceful settlement, and to accept the judgment or award thus obtained. Some advocates of a League of Peace think that the sense of moral obligation in each State, fortified by the public opinion of the civilized world, would form a valid sanction for the fulfilment of such undertakings, and would afford a satisfactory measure of security. But most hold that it is advisable or essential that the members of such a League should bind themselves to take joint action against any member who breaks the peace.

Assuming that a considerable body of nations entered such a League with good and reliable intentions, how far would it be likely to secure the peace of the world and a reduction of armed preparations? The answer to this question would depend mainly upon the number and status of the Powers constituting the League and their relation to outside nations. If, as is not unlikely, at first only a small number of nations were willing to enter such a League, the extent of the pacific achievement would be proportionately circumscribed. If, say, Britain, France, and the United States entered the League, undertaking to settle all their differences by peaceful methods, such a step, however desirable in itself, would not go far towards securing world-peace or enabling these leagued Powers to reduce their national armaments. This is so obvious that most advocates of the League of Peace urge that the leagued Powers should not confine their undertaking to the peaceful settlement of differences among themselves, but should afford a united defence to any of their members attacked by any outside Power which was unwilling to arbitrate its quarrel. A defensive alliance of three such Great Powers (for that is what the League of Peace would amount to at this stage of development) would no doubt form a force which it would be dangerous for any nation, or combination of nations, to attack. But it would secure neither peace nor disarmament. Nor would it, as an earnest advocate of this procedure argues,[1] necessarily, or even probably, form a nucleus of a larger League drawing in other nations. A few nations forming such a League would not differ substantially from the other nominally defensive alliances with which the pages of history are filled. Their purely defensive character would be suspected by outside Powers, who would tend to draw together into an opposing alliance, thus reconstituting once more the Balance of Power with

[1] "Proposals for a League of Peace," by Aneurin Williams, M.P., p. 5.

all its perils and its competing armaments. Nay, if such a League of Peace were constituted in the spirit of the Holy Alliance of a century ago, or of the resurrection of that spirit which Mr. Roosevelt represents in order "to back righteousness by force" in all quarters of the earth, such an opposition of organized outside Powers would be inevitable. The League of Peace idea, in order to have any *prima facie* prospect of success, must at the outset be so planned as to win the adherence of the majority of the Great Powers, including some of those recently engaged in war with one another. For until there was an absolute preponderance of military and naval strength inside the League, the relief from internal strife would do very little, if anything, to abate the total danger of war, or to enable any country to reduce its armed preparations. Further, it would seem essential that such a League should in its relations to outside Powers assume a rigorously defensive attitude, abstaining from all interference in external politics until they encroached directly upon the vital interests of one or more of its members. Such an encroachment it would presumably treat as an attack upon the League, and would afford the injured member such power of redress as was deemed desirable by the representatives of the Powers forming the League.

Before entering upon the fuller consideration of the practicability of a League of Nations formed upon these lines, it may be well to set forth in a brief, formal manner the nature of the chief implications which appear to be contained in the proposal. We shall then be in a position to examine *seriatim* the various steps which the advocates of this method of securing world-peace and disarmament desire to take, and the many difficulties which are involved.

The signatory Powers to the Treaty or Agreement establishing such a League of Peace would undertake :—

(1) To submit to arbitration or conciliation all disputes or differences between them not capable of settlement by ordinary processes of diplomacy, and to accept and carry out any award or terms of settlement thus attained.

(2) To bring joint pressure, diplomatic, economic, or forcible, to bear upon any member refusing to submit a disputed matter to such modes of peaceable settlement, or to accept and carry out the award, or otherwise threatening or opening hostilities against any other member.[1]

(3) To take joint action in repelling any attack made by an outside Power, or group of Powers, upon any of the members of the League.

(4) To take joint action in securing the redress of any injury which, by the general assent of the signatory Powers, had been wrongfully inflicted upon any member of the League.

[1] Many, perhaps most, supporters of a League of Peace would, however, be disposed to apply this police power of the League only in cases where members in contravention of the Treaty actually opened hostilities against another member.

CHAPTER III

INTERNATIONAL ARBITRATION: ITS SCOPE AND METHOD

THE efficacy of a League of Peace, or of any similar arrangement between nations for the prevention of wars and the reduction of armaments, depends, of course, upon the establishment of reliable methods of pacific settlement for all sorts of international differences. The recognition that diplomacy is not always an adequate method of peaceful settlement was the premise from which the Czar's proposal at the International Peace Conference in 1899 proceeded.

"Diplomacy," said M. Staäl, "long ago admitted, among the means of preserving peace, a resort to arbitration and mediation; but it has not defined the conditions of their employment, nor determined the cases to which they are applicable. It is to this high task that we are about to devote our efforts, sustained by the conviction that we are labouring for the welfare of all mankind and in the path marked out for us by preceding generations."

In pursuance of this purpose a Permanent Court of Arbitration has been established at The Hague, to which a number of disputes have been referred for settlement, while an International Prize Court has been set up as a court of appeal from national courts in cases of merchant ships captured in naval warfare. Why should not a group of nations agree to submit either to a court of arbitration or to another judicial tribunal [1] all disputes likely to endanger peace? Arbitration has sometimes been assumed to be a process competent to the pacific settlement of every sort of difference. Treaties have actually been made by which nations have bound themselves to submit all issues without exception to this mode of settlement. In 1898 (before the first Hague Conference) Argentina and Italy had taken this step, and they were followed in 1904 by Denmark's three treaties with Holland, Italy, and Portugal. Theoretically, indeed, no clear distinction can be drawn which should exclude from arbitral settlement any sort of differences arising between nations. "There is no doubt," holds Professor Oppenheim, "that, the consent of the parties once given, every possible difference might be settled through arbitration, whether the verdict is based on the rules of International Law, or rules of national equity, or the opposing claims are compromised." [2] But it does not follow that arbitration is equally suitable or convenient for the settlement of all cases, and at the Hague Conferences and elsewhere a practically useful and generally accepted distinction has been drawn between issues that can best be dealt with by arbitration and issues

[1] Such as the Court of Arbitral Justice proposed by the United States in the Conference of 1907.

[2] "International Law," vol. ii. p. 18.

for which some other method of pacific settlement is better fitted.

It is agreed that differences of a "judicial" or "legal" nature are, in default of any Court of International Justice, especially fitted for arbitral settlement. The Hague Convention embodies this view in Article 16: "The signatory Powers, therein recognizing arbitration as the most efficacious and at the same time most equitable means of determining differences of a judicial character in general, and in especial differences regarding the interpretation or application of international treaties," etc. The phrase used to describe the subjects submitted to arbitration in the Arbitration Treaty between the United States and Great Britain, which lapsed in 1914, was "differences of a legal nature." A distinctly broader sense, however, is assigned to arbitration in the treaties which President Taft endeavoured to negotiate between the United States and various European nations. The term then adopted by Mr. Knox in defining the issues suitable for arbitration was "justiciable," and the form of the treaties ran as follows: "The differences . . . relating to international matters in which the high contracting parties are concerned by virtue of a claim of right made by one against the other under treaty or otherwise, and which are justiciable in their nature by reason of being susceptible of decision by the application of the principles of law or equity," etc.

Ex-President Taft's interpretation of this language deserves citation. "First, the differences must relate to international affairs; second, they arise upon a claim of right—i.e. a right under a treaty or under principles of international law of one against the other; third, they must be justiciable—i.e. capable of judicial solution by application of the principles of law or equity."[1]

Now this definition evidently excludes certain causes of dissension and dispute between nations as unsuitable for this mode of settlement. Strained relations between nations sometimes occur when no international injury is alleged and no "claim of right" arises, as, for example, where the members of one nation are resentful at the persecution of their co-religionists or co-racials by the Government of another nation. More numerous are the quarrels when the commercial policy of one nation inflicts grave injury upon the commerce of another, though, as in the case of Tariffs, there is no question as to the "right" of the offender to pursue this policy. Mr. Taft's definition would also exclude political issues of a "general" order such as could not be brought down to any definite point of law or fact, such issues as are involved in the rival claims for spheres of influence, the competition in armaments, the acquisition of railroad concessions in territory where the acquiring Power obtains an important strategical advantage over a neighbour, etc.

Finally, the confinement to "the application of the principles of law or equity" excludes disputes turning wholly upon questions of fact.

Now if we are seeking means for composing every sort of dispute or ill-feeling between nations, we shall evidently require several different methods

[1] "The United States and Peace," p. 107.

of procedure accommodated to the nature of the trouble.

It is pretty evident that the various disputes can be brought under three categories: disputes of law and its application, disputes of fact not involving law, and disputes of policy. Dr. Marburg deduces from this distinction three modes of treatment. "Diplomacy, including good offices and mediation, may, of course, deal with all of them. But the finding of facts is naturally the function of a commission of inquiry or jury, while the determination of law and its application falls properly within the province of a court of law. Disputes as to policy are the only ones which, after the failure of diplomacy to compose them, lean naturally for final settlement on arbitration, the inherent principle of which is compromise." [1] Of the logical validity and the practical utility of this distinction there can be no question. There will be, of course, some overlapping or mingling of these issues. There will be mixed questions of fact and law, and questions of policy which can in part at any rate be resolved into questions of fact. But if we were building with a free hand our structure of international agreement, we should certainly establish a separate International Judicature for the determination of points of law, a Commission of Inquiry to discover facts, and a Conciliation or Arbitration Court to compose disputes of a political or general character.

But the separation of the distinctively judicial from the arbitration process is not easy to com-

[1] "Law and Judicial Settlement," Dr. Marburg, No. 18. "Judicial Settlement of International Disputes."

pass. Two difficulties may render it impossible in the beginnings of international architecture. The formal establishment of an International Judicature would seem to, and would, in fact, involve an acknowledgment on the part of sovereign States of a more definite cession of sovereignty than they may be willing to consent to. Moreover, the sharp distinction between judicial procedure and arbitration has not been maintained even by its advocates at The Hague or elsewhere. This is conclusively shown by reference to the title Court of Arbitral Justice, which the American delegates at the Second Hague Conference proposed to substitute for the existing Court of Arbitration. In urging the establishment of this Court, neither the American nor the other supporters sought to distinguish the judicial from the arbitrable disputes, but confined their advocacy to emphasizing the greater continuity and other advantages attendant upon the reform.

Moreover, though Mr. Taft in the passage above quoted drew a sharp distinction between justiciable and non-justiciable cases, elsewhere he seems willing to bring all definitely "international" issues under the arbitral process.[1]

In view of these facts and of the further fact that in the existing international treaties for settle-

[1] "My whole ideal is that of an arbitral court for the settlement of international controversies, and I favoured the arbitration treaties as a long step towards an arbitral court whose jurisdiction should be increased ultimately to include all possible disputes of an international character."—Letter to Conference of American Society for Judicial Settlement of International Disputes, 1914.

ment of disputes no distinction between judicial and arbitrable is known, the cases of interpretation and application of international law being recognized as suitable for arbitration, it may be well for our present discussion to ignore this distinction of Dr. Marburg, and to adhere to our preliminary division into arbitrable and non-arbitrable issues.

Now, this division involves a withdrawal of the strict division between issues of law and issues of fact. Even in national judicial procedure the distinction cannot always be preserved, and in many instances the judge determines the latter as well as the former. In the actual history of arbitration the ascertainment of definite crucial facts has always formed an acknowledged part of the arbitrator's work.

The most serviceable distinction between arbitrable and non-arbitrable cases is made by another American lawyer, who says: "There cannot be an arbitrable question unless there is a dispute between nations as to some questions of fact or some question of international law. Purely political or dogmatic questions cannot in their nature be arbitrated." [1] Without entering further into the subtleties of the question, we can, I think, form a pretty clear idea of the kinds of issue that are conveniently arbitrable.

First, all disputes as to the interpretation or application of treaties or other formal agreements between nations.

Secondly, disputes capable of settlement by the

[1] Mr. Hornblower, "Report of a Conference on Judicial Settlement of International Disputes, 1913," p. 213.

application of the principles of international law.[1]

Thirdly, disputes on questions of fact that are capable of submission to ordinary processes of legal evidence.

It is the third class that raises the most difficulty. All differences are in a sense dependent on questions of fact. The question how far Germany intended to bring about this war, and what her motives were, the question whether France made her Russian alliance in order some day to carry out a war of *revanche*, whether Russia's stiffening on the Servian grievance was due to her recognition that the time was ripe—these are questions of fact. But such inner facts of feeling and intention cannot be ascertained by arbitration with any measure of certainty.

Disputes of fact for purposes of arbitration must relate to concrete facts, or motives which in the nature of the case are clearly ascertainable by evidence of facts. Whether a vessel struck a rock or was destroyed by a mine, whether a Government authorized a punitive expedition across a distant frontier, what amount of damages would cover the injuries sustained by the illegal launching of the *Alabama*—such ascertainments of fact and measurable valuations upon evidence are eminently fit for arbitration. This, however, does not exclude all cases of subjective fact or intention. The fixation of responsibility, as well as the extent of injury, may be determined by arbitration. The

[1] International law differs from municipal law in that it is not the creation of any Legislature or of any judicial process. It is nothing other than recognized international usage.

Report of the Dogger Bank Commission was in effect, and might have been in form, an arbitral award, though it was the result of what was described as an "Inquiry."

But adopting provisionally the distinction which confines arbitration disputes to the questions of interpretation, law, and fact, just enumerated, we find among statesmen a great reluctance to consent to submit to arbitration all issues that are in these senses arbitrable. No arbitration treaty has been made between two Great Powers in which all differences of a legal nature are submitted. Differences affecting "vital interests," "honour," and "independence" are excepted. These were the exceptions in the series of treaties made by Great Britain in 1903 and 1904 with France, Spain, Italy, Germany, Sweden, Norway, Portugal, and Austria-Hungary. To these exceptions "territorial integrity" is sometimes added. The reservations made by the Senate of the United States in the treaties of general arbitration proposed by Mr. Knox, specified in addition to "territorial integrity" questions relating to the admission and treatment of "aliens," and the indebtedness of a State, and all issues relating to the Monroe doctrine of foreign policy.[1]

[1] The American proposal for an obligatory world treaty of arbitration in a general form, submitted to the Hague Conference of 1907, took the following shape: "Differences of a judicial kind, and before all those relating to the interpretation of treaties existing between two or more of the contracting States, which may arise between the said States in the future, and which shall not have been settled by diplomatic means, shall be submitted to arbitration, on the condition that they affect neither the vital interests nor the independence or honour of

It is, of course, apparent that "honour" and "vital interests" can be made to cover almost any issue of sufficient importance to endanger the peace between nations, and that the formal exclusion of such issues renders arbitration treaties of comparatively little worth as a provision against war. The retention of such reservations virtually cancels the so-called obligation to submit to arbitration any class of issues named in the treaty. It is, however, needless to labour so obvious a point. If arbitration is to be made an effective method for securing peace, all issues in their nature arbitrable must be brought within its scope, irrespective of their importance or the feeling that attaches to them. The question, for example, of the alleged complicity of the Servian Government in the Serajevo assassination, affecting, as it undoubtedly did, both honour and vital interests, was eminently suitable for arbitral decision.

But if arbitration is to be made a really effective international instrument for peace, it is not enough that individual nations should bind themselves to refer to arbitration all issues that are arbitrable, including those affecting honour and vital interests. Such a network of separate treaties ought to be replaced by a general treaty to which all the Powers should set their signature. The efforts of several Powers to induce the representatives at the 1907 Hague Conference to enter a general treaty were defeated by the fact that no prior

either of the said States, and that they do not affect the interests of other States not parties to the controversy." The decision as to the relation of any case to honour, vital interests, or independence is left to the several signatory Powers.

agreement had yet been reached among the Powers to submit to arbitration all justiciable issues. All sorts of divergences were disclosed as to the kinds of issues which particular States were or were not willing to arbitrate. So long as the several States insisted on considering the proposal of compulsory arbitration in the particular light of their own national interests and history, disregarding or insufficiently regarding their larger interest in maintaining the peace of the world, the conditions of a general treaty, as distinct from separate treaties, were not attainable. This objection was promptly and persistently maintained by the representatives of Germany. Baron Marschall von Bieberstein put the matter in the following way :—

"It would be an error to believe that a general arbitrational agreement concluded between two States can serve purely and simply as a model, or, so to speak, a formulary for a world-treaty. The matter is very different in the two cases. Between two States which conclude a treaty of general obligatory arbitration, the field of possible differences is more or less under the eyes of the treaty members ; it is circumscribed by a series of concrete and familiar factors, such as the geographical situation of the two countries, their financial and economic relations, and the historic traditions which have grown up between them. In a treaty including all the countries of the world, these concrete factors are wanting, and hence, even in the restricted list of juristic questions, the possibility of differences of every kind is illimitable. It follows from this that a general arbitrational agreement which, between two States, defines with sufficient clearness the rights and duties which flow from it, might be in a world-treaty too vague and elastic, and therefore inapplicable." [1]

The discussions of the Conference, which, after abandoning the attempt to define the subjects of arbitration by exclusion, endeavoured to secure agreement upon a specified list of subjects for inclusion, supported this criticism of von Bieberstein. The attempt to secure general acceptance for an agreed list of subjects proper for arbitration by a general treaty completely failed. A careful list of subjects, founded upon actual treaties recently negotiated, was most harshly treated by the Conference. "Of the twenty-four clauses voted on, only the first eight received a majority of the votes of the Committee ; of the eighteen countries represented on the Committee, from four to nine cast adverse votes in each case. Two delegates (Germany and Austria) voted against every one of the clauses ; and two others (Belgium and Greece) either voted against every one or abstained from voting at all ; while only five (France, Norway, the Netherlands, Portugal, and Servia) voted for all of them." [2]

It seems evident that no such general treaty of arbitration as seems essential to the formation of an effective League of Nations will be possible unless the signatory Powers are willing to submit all arbitrable issues, inclusive of those affecting honour and vital interests. So long as the spirit of reserve prevails, inducing each nation to seek to exclude some set of issues of

[1] Quoted, Hull, *The Two Hague Conferences*, p. 313.

[2] Hull, p. 334.

special interest to itself, a general treaty must prove impracticable. It is perhaps possible that a new spirit may prevail among those who are sent to represent the nations at the settlement of this war. Might it not be felt that the honour and the vital interests of a nation are better conserved by accepting an award impartially decided on the merits of the case than by insisting on the ordeal of battle?

It may seem to some a matter of light importance whether nations seeking peaceable relations with their neighbours bind themselves by separate treaties in each instance, or participate in a general arbitration treaty. But sound internationalism demands the latter process. So long as the policy of special treaties holds, the tendency to negotiate them only with certain favoured or favourable nations, and to pay regard to particular objects in the way of inclusion or exclusion, will continue to prevail. Only by assent to a general treaty can the standardization of arbitral justice be secured. Nor does this apply only to the agreements ; it applies also to the process of arbitration. It is a prime requisite for equitable arbitration that the best conditions for complete impartiality, as regards the constitution of the Court and its methods of procedure, shall prevail. These conditions are better fulfilled where every case that arises proceeds automatically to a standing tribunal, with a skilled personnel of experienced judges following a recognized procedure, than where special arrangements may be made by the two parties for a tribunal of their own selection. The damage done to the reputation of arbitration by the appointment of arbitrators who are, in fact, *ex parte* advocates, and whose ultimate awards carry a recognizable bias, has been considerable. Compromise is essential to arbitration. But there is every difference between a compromise which embodies the spirit of give and take, or mutual concession, and that which is the mechanical register or resultant of a number of opposing pulls.

Such an extension of the existing scope of arbitration, and such a tightening of the arbitral apparatus at The Hague, would virtually accomplish the work to which the representatives of the United States especially addressed themselves in the Hague Conference of 1907, viz: the substitution of a permanent Court of Arbitral Justice for the loosely composed Arbitration Court already in being. The chief defects of the existing structure were thus designated by Mr. Choate :—

"The fact that there was nothing permanent or continuous or connected in the sessions of the Court, or in the adjudication of the cases submitted to it, has been an obvious source of weakness and want of prestige in the tribunal. Each trial it had before it has been wholly independent of every other, and its occasional utterances, widely distant in time and disconnected in subject-matter, have not gone far towards constituting a consistent body of international law or of valuable contributions to international law, which ought to emanate from an international tribunal representing the power and might of all the nations. In fact, it has thus far been a Court only in name, a framework for the selection of referees for each particular case, never consisting of the same judges. It has done great good so far as it has been permitted to work at all, but our effort should be to try to make it the medium of vastly greater and constantly increasing benefit to the nations and mankind at large. Let us, then, seek to develop out of it a Permanent Court which shall hold regular and continuous sessions, which shall consist of the same judges, which shall pay due heed to its own decisions, which shall speak with the authority of the united voice of the nations and gradually build up a system of international law, definite and precise, which shall command the approval and regulate the conduct of the nations."

The proposal received powerful support, not only from the Russian representatives, who had themselves drafted a similar proposal, but from Baron von Bieberstein on behalf of Germany. Such opposition as was invoked to overthrow the acceptance of the scheme arose almost entirely from the small nations, and was directed, not to the essential merits of the proposal but to the structure of the Court that was proposed. The demand of the smaller nations for absolute international equality in the appointment of the judges was the rock on which the proposal split. This fear of the small nations lest a Tribunal, virtually endowed with a legislative power, should operate to secure the practical domination of a few Great Powers cannot be ignored in any practical discussion of arbitration in the more extended form which is required. This risk might, no doubt, be obviated, in part at any rate, by strictly circumscribing the jurisdiction of the Court so as to confine its powers within the limits set by the original agreement. It is, however, right to recognize that the acceptance of the claim to equality made by the small Powers would be likely to prove a stout obstacle to the adhesion of certain Great Powers, especially if the scope of arbitral justice were extended to include, not merely the minor concrete issues hitherto submitted, but all arbitrable issues involving honour and vital interests.

But leaving on one side for the present these grave political difficulties relating to the composition of the tribunal, the proposed enlargement of the powers and consolidation of the structure of the Hague Court would seem essential to the full and effective work of arbitration. It is desirable, then, that in the settlement of this war every effort should be made to induce the Powers to bind themselves to submit to that process all issues of an arbitrable nature, and to enter into a general treaty for the establishment of a permanent Tribunal of Arbitral Justice before which all such cases should be tried.

CHAPTER IV

SETTLEMENT BY CONCILIATION

WHAT is to be done for the pacific settlement of such differences as are in their nature not suited for arbitration? Purely political or dynastic questions, we have already recognized, cannot be arbitrated. Many, if not most, of the issues fraught with greatest peril to peace are of this order. They sometimes consist in a general attitude of policy or in inflammation of feeling which cannot be reduced to definite claims or complaints, and is not compassed in any clearly specified acts. The danger always simmering in the Balkans has largely been of this general character, though taking concrete local shape at various moments. The intrigues of Austria and of Russia among these East European States could scarcely ever be formulated in a manner suitable for arbitration. The resentment and suspicion of the growing military power of Germany or Russia by other nations, and fears relating to a disturbance of the Balance of Power, the ill-feeling evoked in one nation by the sudden adoption by another nation of a tariff, apparently designed to damage the trade of the former nation, the question of competition for spheres of influence in China or in other parts of Asia, the whole grave issue of competition in armaments, belong to a class of differences which cannot in their main aspect be brought to arbitration.

Again, there are matters of difference not directly contained in any political act or attitude, and to the settlement of which no existing international law is applicable. Many points in the working of the postal, telegraphic, monetary systems which are essential to international intercourse, rules relating to phyloxera, rinderpest, and other pests, common regulations for protection of life and property at sea, the standardization of weights and measures, alien immigration and repatriation where no formal treaties exist, and a great variety of other issues which are either unsuitable for international law or treaty, or which are not, in fact, brought under these processes—all such issues are liable to contain inflammatory matter which may not be strictly arbitrable in its nature.

Discussion at The Hague in 1907 showed how impossible it was to obtain any agreement among the Powers as to the inclusion of such questions in a general treaty of arbitration. For though some of the opposition to the several items was based upon an objection either to the "obligatory" or to the "general" principle of a world-treaty, there was a genuine and widespread conviction that many of these disputes were not truly "arbitrable," at any rate in the shape in which they would first arise. The underlying objection was that most of them involved issues of policy.

Now, what is to be done with these non-arbitrable issues? They are often the more dangerous because they are not reducible to sharp questions of law or fact. America has always rightly recognized that the Monroe Doctrine was not suitable for arbitration. No principles of a Court of Arbitration could deal satisfactorily with Germany's demand for "colonial expansion" or "a place in the sun," or with the political feelings and pressures contained in Pan-Slavism. The intricacy, intellectual vagueness, inflamed emotionalism which characterize such issues demand that some other process than arbitration be applied, at any rate in the first instance. To give any reasonable prospect of adjusting bad relations of this kind, it is first advisable to endeavour to make the grievances or demands which they contain more explicit. To give them substance and clear significance by ascertaining facts and obtaining a statement of demands or complaints and their counterclaims would be the first stage in a process of adjustment.

A timely inquiry into such discussions or grievances, held by an impartial body, might evidently be of service, either for obtaining a settlement by diplomatic agreement or by stating a case suitable for arbitration. This object it was sought to obtain at the Hague Conference of 1899 by the adoption of International Commissions of Inquiry under the following conditions: "In differences of an international nature, involving neither honour nor essential interests, and arising from a difference of opinion on matters of fact, the signatory Powers judge it useful that parties who have not been able to come to an agreement by diplomatic negotiations should institute, as far as circumstances permit, an International Commission of Inquiry, charged with aiding in the settlement of disputes by an impartial and thorough investigation and statement of the facts" (Article 9).

Though the terms of the establishment of this procedure leave its application purely optional, and an attempt made by Russia and the United States in 1899 and 1907 to give some authority to the report or award of such an Inquiry was rejected, the existence of this machinery of Inquiry entitled to examine and report upon the facts of a dispute, not in its existing shape capable of settlement by diplomacy or arbitration, clearly indicates the line of procedure along which we may go in seeking a pacific settlement for all issues adjudged not suitable for arbitration.

But if this instrument is to be really serviceable, its uses and powers must be amended and amplified. The proposal made by Professor de Maartens [1] to enlarge the Commission's duty of "aiding in the settlement of disputes by an impartial and thorough investigation and statement of the facts" by adding the further duty of "fixing, if necessary, the responsibility for the facts" is indispensable to a really serviceable "award."

What is needed is, first, to enlarge the scope of the Commission of Inquiry, so as to bring within its purview all international disputes or difficulties not considered suitable for arbitration ; secondly, to make the submission of such issues compulsory ; thirdly, to substitute a general for all particular

[1] Hull, 291.

treaties of reference; fourthly, to convert the reports of fact when necessary into an award; and finally, to procure for that award the sanction requisite to secure its acceptance by the parties concerned.

In a word, Inquiry should be a preliminary process for Conciliation, and the award of the Inquiry should be made the basis of a settlement as valid as that attached to the award of the Arbitration Court. Indeed, it is clear that the relation between the Conciliation process and the Arbitration Court must be one of close co-operation. For in not a few instances the process of Inquiry may be confined to the bare ascertainment of such facts as make a concrete case to be stated for the Arbitration Court. In other words, it must be competent upon a fully equipped Council of Conciliation either to issue an award and endeavour by such powers of pressure as may be assigned to it to obtain its acceptance or some satisfactory compromise, or else to hand over the matter stated in a form suitable for some arbitral or other tribunal to determine.

Since it has been admitted that it may be convenient to include in the functions of the Arbitration Court some issues not of law or interpretation of international obligations but of fact, it may be well to indicate more clearly what sorts of issues of fact may be left for arbitration and what properly belong to the Inquiry or Conciliation process. The issues of fact left to arbitration would be such facts as in reference to a concrete case would in a court of justice be held competent for a jury to decide. There are, however, two sorts of inquiry into facts better undertaken by a different method. Questions of international finance and commerce often involve expert knowledge and minute work of investigation best performed by a specially appointed Commission of Inquiry. The same is true of many matters relating to the use of the high seas for transport and for fishing, the standardization of weights and measures, epidemics, and other hygienic matters, international co-operation for meteorological and other scientific services, and for ascertaining many other sorts of knowledge requisite as a foundation for international legislation. Such matters of inquiry do not necessarily involve disputes or ill-feeling, though they are often liable to produce such friction. But they all relate to questions of common interest among nations which require for their settlement some more or less expert processes of investigation and judgment.

The other sorts of facts demanding inquiry are those embedded in the large, vague, heated controversies or discussions which we have recognized cannot in their crude state be submitted for arbitration. The Balkan situation, the West-Asiatic railway problem, or the more general aspects of the international interests in Morocco, Egypt, Persia, China, are not suitable for the handling of an Arbitration Court. But a patient, impartial international Inquiry, could it be arranged, might discover, extract, and formulate certain concrete issues relating to the claims, fears, and interests of the several parties, which might then form fit matter for arbitration.

It is, however, evident that a mere Inquiry and

report on facts is not all that requires to be done. Powers of Conciliation must be definitely associated with the process of Inquiry if a real alternative to Arbitration is to be established.

The most important experiment in this direction is provided in the form of the Permanent International Commissions set up by the treaties concluded in the autumn of 1914 by the United States with Great Britain and with France. The treaty [1] between the United States and the United Kingdom, ratified on November 14, 1914, established a "Peace Commission" for inquiry into and report upon all disputes not covered by existing agreements.

Its chief operative Articles read as follows: "The High Contracting Parties agree that all disputes between them, of every nature whatsoever, other than disputes the settlement of which is provided for, and in fact achieved, under existing agreements between the High Contracting Parties, shall, when diplomatic methods of adjustment have failed, be referred for investigation and report to a Permanent International Commission to be constituted in the manner prescribed in the next succeeding article; and they agree not to declare war or begin hostilities during such investigation and before the report is submitted." [2]

"The International Commission shall be composed of five members, to be appointed as follows: one member shall be drawn from each country by the Government thereof; one member shall be chosen by each Government from some third country; the fifth shall be chosen by common

[1] Cd. 7714.

[2] Article I.

agreement between the two Governments, it being understood that he shall not be a citizen of either country." [1]

"In case the High Contracting Parties shall have failed to adjust a dispute by diplomatic methods, they shall at once refer it to the International Commission for investigation and report. The International Commission may, however, offer its services to that effect, and in such case it shall notify both Governments and request their co-operation in the investigation." [2]

The Parties agree to furnish "all the means and facilities required for its investigation and report." The Report is to be completed within a year from the beginning of the investigation, unless both Parties agree on the extension or restriction of the term.

Though in form this procedure is simply one of investigation, its evident purpose and result are to produce an atmosphere and other conditions favourable to conciliation. The year's delay exerts a cooling and a healing effect, allowing time for the facts disclosed by a full impartial inquiry to make their right impression on the intelligence of the disputants, while it likewise informs the public opinion and directs the judgment and sympathy of the neutral world. Controversies thus dragged from the mists of ignorance and passion into the light of established truth and right will more easily admit of peaceful settlement, and any refusal to settle in conformity with what appears to the outside world the plain direction of reason and justice will become continually more difficult to maintain.

[1] Article II. [2] Article III.

The influence of the neutral world will be immensely strengthened by the consciousness of the possession of full and reliable knowledge of the facts.

It is true that the parties only bind themselves to an Inquiry and a period of peaceable delay, and that the report of the Commission does not in form constitute an award, or involve any express obligation upon the parties to take any line of action. What it does is to provide, after a cooling-off time, a reasoned, pacific statement of the case with such suggestions for a verdict or a compromise as are involved in every clear judicial summary. It supplies the atmosphere and the materials for fresh conciliation, leaving liberty to the parties, after the report is given, to reopen diplomatic negotiations under these new conditions.

How far does this method meet our requirements for a peaceful settlement of non-arbitrable issues? In addition to the great intrinsic merits which we have already recognized, there are several others deserving attention. In the first place, there is no exclusion of issues from the Commission of Inquiry on grounds of honour, vital interests, or any other account. In the second place, there is the right accorded to the Commission of taking the initiative in instituting an Inquiry. This initiative is of immeasurable value in the development of adequate processes of peaceful settlement. For by bringing forward for investigation matters of international dissension before they have ripened into issues of political dispute, much heat and danger would be averted. A well-informed Commission, spying a cloud when it was no bigger than a man's hand, might stop many a storm.

Finally, the permanent character of this Commission is a notable improvement upon the *ad hoc* method of appointment, or even the selection from a panel, which often taints a process of Inquiry from the beginning with doubts relating to the competence or the impartiality of the personnel.

But, excellent as are the provisions of this Peace Commission, it falls short in several important respects of the full requirements of a machinery for the settlement of non-arbitrable issues.

In the first place, there is no security that such a Commission will interpret its functions so liberally as to furnish a report which is of necessity and in substance an award or judgment. A merely impartial sifting of evidence and summary of facts, though highly serviceable, would only furnish an opportunity for reopening diplomatic discussion towards an amicable settlement, which might not after all be attained. There is in the Treaty no provision for a genuine award, and none for a direct invitation to Conciliation. An amplification of the functions of the Commission of Inquiry, so as to convert it into a Commission of Conciliation, is required. The report should be, so far as possible, a genuine award, containing proposals for an equitable settlement, and representatives of the Governments concerned should be brought together in order that they may agree either to accept and carry out the award, or to adopt some other settlement, or failing either of these courses, to state a case for arbitral settlement.

By some such extension of functions the Peace

Commission could be developed into a Council of Conciliation, which, taken in conjunction with the Court of Arbitration or of Arbitral Justice, would furnish a mode of peaceful settlement for all disputes not capable of diplomatic arrangement. What is needed is that the Powers should bind themselves to the settlement of all issues by some method other than arms. The obligation to submit the case to investigation is not enough, unless it is accompanied by an obligation either to abide by the results of the investigation or to adopt some other pacific arrangement.

A compact and workable machinery for pacific settlement will, of course, require that, as in the case of Arbitration, so here, all the consenting States should be brought into a single Treaty for Investigation and Conciliation. This will have not only the obvious advantage of unifying the pacific arrangements of the world, but it will also improve the structure of the Commission for all work of expert and impartial inquiry by affording a larger choice of men and a larger area for the collection and standardization of authoritative facts. A Council of Inquiry and Conciliation, upon which most of the civilized nations of the earth were represented, would probably substitute for the method of appointment in this Anglo-American Treaty another which not only would secure completer and more evident impartiality, but would by this very character mobilize for the execution of the award a far more general consensus of public sentiment throughout the civilized world.

Reserving, however, for later consideration this important question of the composition and appointment of the Council of Conciliation, and the similar question in relation to the Court of Arbitration, we must briefly discuss the way in which disputes may best be brought into these processes of pacific settlement. Here are two related questions, that of initiation and that of determination of competency. If disputes are at some stage before danger-point is reached, to be removed from diplomatic controversy for inquiry and settlement before a Court of Arbitration or a Council of Conciliation, it will not suffice to leave this action to the motion of the contestants alone. For if it is left to the two Governments to agree upon such a reference they may fail to do so, and the dispute may drag on with grave present injury and the danger of a sudden outbreak of public passion in one or both nations, which may either lead to violent action, or may otherwise render any subsequent process of pacific settlement more difficult. Even were they led to an agreement either to arbitrate or to conciliate their differences, their choice between these processes might not be a good one. On the other hand, it would not be sufficient to confer upon any single interested party the right to appeal to Arbitration or Conciliation and thereby compel the other reluctantly to come in. For though it might be well to have this power of joint or several initiation on the part of the contestant parties as the ordinary method of procedure, it would be desirable that a separate power of initiation should be vested in the Arbitration or Conciliation bodies themselves or in some other Court of First Instance.

We have already assigned to the Council of Conciliation the duty of exercising an initiative of inquiry into important and delicate issues which are not in their existing form matters of definite dispute or difference. But in dealing with actual matters or conditions of international friction, it would probably be best to leave the initial action to a Joint Standing Committee representing the two Arbitration and Conciliation bodies, unless some such further development of international government as we discuss later is found practicable. The functions of such a Committee would be to watch the course of gathering controversies and, in default of an appeal from one or both of the parties concerned, to invite them to appear before a preliminary inquiry, the objects of which should be to ascertain whether the matter was suitable for settlement in Arbitration or for submission to the freer process of investigation and report employed by the Conciliation Council. The Treaty establishing a League of Nations would, therefore, in the first instance, bind the signatory Powers, not to a particular mode of settlement by Arbitration or otherwise, but to submit all issues on request to a Joint Committee of Investigation, empowered to determine whether the particular issue was by reason of its nature, or the point of its development, suitable for settlement by Arbitration or Conciliation, or by a preliminary process of Inquiry by the Council of Conciliation with a view to subsequent reference to Arbitration.[1] The essential point in such a Treaty would be to bind the

[1] It would, however, probably be right that the Arbitration Court should retain a final right of veto upon matters submitted to them as arbitrable.

Powers to refrain from acts of hostility, and to entrust to the representative Commission the duty of determining what process of pacific settlement among those provided by the Treaty should in each case be adopted. The signatory Powers would then undertake, first, to have recourse to this Joint Committee for a preliminary inquiry ; secondly, to submit their case to such process of Arbitration or Conciliation as the Joint Committee might determine to be applicable to the case ; and thirdly, to accept the award or report of either of these processes as a basis of settlement, refraining in the meantime from any act or preparation of hostility.

Such would be the substance of a League constructed on the basis of furnishing adequate and appropriate organs of pacific settlement in impartial and representative international bodies.

If the majority of civilized States, including most of the Great Powers, were willing to enter such a League, and possessed sufficient confidence in the justice and efficiency of its procedure and in its ability to secure submission to its awards, not merely would the cause of peace be greatly advanced but the question of reduction of armaments would for the first time come within the range of practical politics. For the play of militant motives would now be reversed. The aggressive motive for armaments would be weakened by the recognition that acts of aggression were no longer feasible, the defensive motive by the recognition that the full defence of each nation no longer devolved upon its own armed resources or those of its few temporary allies.

Under such conditions the difficulties which would seem to beset the attempt to find a basis for agreed reduction of armaments would largely disappear. Motives of national economy would tend to prevail in each of the confederates, and so powerful an impulse towards disarmament might by given in some instances that the agreement upon armaments which would form a natural adjunct of the Treaty establishing the League might have to bind the signatories to maintain a proper quota of military and naval forces for common purposes of defence.

The efficiency of such a League of Peace and the establishment of the necessary confidence in its lasting power to fulfil its pacific functions would depend mainly upon three considerations which now await discussion. First, the appointment and composition of the Court of Arbitration and the Council of Inquiry and Conciliation. Secondly, the powers wielded by the League to secure the fulfilment of the undertakings of the Powers to submit all issues to pacific settlement and to accept and carry out the awards of the Court and Council. Thirdly, such changes in the conduct of diplomacy and of international politics, especially in trade and finance, as will expel those antagonisms of interest which have been the chief feeders of enmity, jealousy, and mutual suspicion.

CHAPTER V

COURT AND COUNCIL: THEIR APPOINTMENT AND PERSONNEL

THE proposal to resort to Arbitration and Conciliation for the settlement of all disagreements between nations that cannot be composed by ordinary diplomatic methods will appear to most persons acceptable and feasible because it seems to involve no novel, untried principle, but to be only an extension of existing practices. But while this view is substantially true, it would be foolish to ignore or to extenuate the magnitude of the steps that constitute that extension.

Two great advances must be made if our scheme for the settlement of disputes is to be achieved. The substitution of a general for a number of particular international agreements, and the establishment of a genuinely international Court of Arbitration and Council of Inquiry and Conciliation, mark the first great advance towards international regulation. Existing agreements for arbitration and conciliation are contained in a great number and variety of treaties between separate pairs of nations, and the personal constitution of the courts which they provide is in most instances determined by the interested parties. The Arbitral Court at The Hague was indeed constituted at the first Conference on a wide international basis, but the actual tribunal appointed to try a case between two nations was composed of two nominees of each nation out of the international panel, with an umpire drawn by agreement of the two parties, or, failing that, by a third person selected by the parties. This same method was also adopted for a Commission of Inquiry. Though it was permissible for the parties in dispute to agree upon any other method of selecting a tribunal out of the members of the Permanent Court, it was expected that the members chosen by each party would be members of their own nationality nominated by them to serve on the Court, or members of some other nationality that owed their nomination to the party now calling on their services. Though the Conference of 1907 modified this interested method of appointment, by providing that only one of the two arbitrators selected by each nation may be a citizen of the country that selected him, or an original nominee of that country, the fact that the actual constitution of the Tribunal was fixed by the selecting of persons supposed by the two parties respectively to be favourably disposed to their case clearly derogates from the international impartiality of the proceedings. The same criticism applies to the Commission of Inquiry, whether as established by the Hague Convention or, as in the case of the American Treaties already concluded, by the two parties undertaking to submit their disputes to a specially constituted Commission.

If these processes are to become generally and fully international, both the form of the treaty and the constitution of the Court or Commission must bear the impress, not of separate arrangements between pairs of Powers each playing for its own hand, but of a procedure informed throughout by the wider international spirit. This can be best accomplished by inviting the Powers to enter one general obligatory treaty referring their disputes to such a Court or Council, and leaving to that Court or Council as a whole the appointment of the personnel of the body adjudicating or inquiring into each matter of dispute.

It may, of course, be difficult for certain Powers to consent to enter upon any process of settlement where their own representatives will only at the most possess a minority voice. But if full confidence is to be secured for the impartiality of such a process, the axiom of justice that no one can be a judge of his own case must be observed. This reform of constitution and procedure would have another very salutary effect. So long as a case of arbitration or inquiry is conducted by a body which, as regards the majority of its members, is in composition partisan, the justice of the matter is always in danger of being subordinated either to a test of strength or to the conditions of a compromise indefensible in principle and contributing nothing to the body of international law or sound usage. Nations engaging to submit their disputes to such a process will always incline to appoint as their representatives upon the panel of the Court or Council able advocates who will be expected to champion their cause, and though the permanency of the constitution of these bodies may give some independence to the personnel in dealing with particular cases, the patriotic bias will always come into suspicion.

Still more important is this consideration in its bearing on the type of person which the several Powers appoint as their representatives. Here a distinction may be drawn between the Arbitral Court and the Conciliation Council in virtue of the different nature of their work. The functions of the former being distinctively judicial, it would seem natural and proper that men of legal eminence and conversant with international law should usually be appointed. But the composition of the Council of Conciliation requires a different sort of representative. The inquiries it will be called upon to undertake will often be broader in scope, more delicate in subject-matter, and less susceptible to definite awards than the cases which come before the Arbitral Court. A large discretion must be accorded to its methods of inquiry, which should not be closely governed by legal rules or usages. Conciliation being the end, the report of such an Inquiry will be presented, not usually in the shape of a definite judgment or award, but as a summary of evidence with an opinion given in the form of suggestions for one or more modes of settlement. Not infrequently the report of the Inquiry might take shape in a statement of a case for Arbitration. The direct value and weight of such a report, and the willingness of the parties to adopt it as a basis for diplomatic settlement, must evidently depend upon the measure of intellectual and moral authority which the character and procedure of the Council can command. For whatever sanction or support can be devised for this process of Conciliation, the recommendations which its report may contain cannot in themselves possess the force of the judicial decision or the definite award of the Arbitration Court, nor can they be defended as a logically sound application of recognized rules of international law. In other words, the value of Conciliation depends more upon the personal independence, ability, discretion, and integrity of the members of the Council than in the case of Arbitration. Moreover, we recognize that the most dangerous disputes are likely to come up, at all events in the first instance, before the Council rather than the Arbitration Court. It is therefore essential that the members drawn for this process shall, so far as possible, not merely possess the high personal qualifications mentioned above, but shall be known by the world at large, and especially by their fellow-countrymen, to possess them. For the essential meaning of Conciliation is peaceful persuasion, and the recommendations of the Council will therefore depend for their efficacy upon the influence they exercise, first upon public opinion in the nations directly affected by the dispute or difference for which a peaceful settlement is sought, and secondly, upon the wider judgment of the society of nations represented in the Council. The crucial test of the efficacy of the process will be the voluntary acceptance by a nation of recommendations that are adverse to its former claims and interests because of its confidence in the impartiality and efficiency of the

Inquiry, and its recognition that the recommendations command the general assent of disinterested nations.

It is, of course, impossible to expect at the outset of such an experiment in internationalism that an ideally constituted Council of men of international mind will be obtained. There will be a tendency among most nations to appoint members who can be relied upon to represent effectively upon the Board the particular interests and points of view of their nation. Nor is this disposition wholly to be reprobated. The sentiment and intellectual attitude of genuine internationalism can only be acquired and confirmed by actual experience in international co-operation. Until the needed experience is got, the internationalism of such a Council must be somewhat inchoate and mechanical, an equilibrium of national interests and feelings rather than a positively international mind. It is this consideration that makes it so important to substitute a general treaty for specific treaties between pairs of nations, and to substitute for Courts and Commissions manned by representatives of the contestant nations bodies that are genuinely international in composition. For the suspicion and the self-regarding nationalism which express themselves at first in the selection of reliable nationalists rather than of completely impartial men for representatives on international Court and Council, will gradually disappear when it is realized that the forms of procedure as well as the spirit are framed so as to educate the international mind. It will, however, continue to be important that the representatives of any nation on the Council should be men commanding the high respect of their fellow-countrymen. For, in the first place, this will be essential to secure for them their proper status on the Council, and secondly, it will enable them the better to ensure the fair consideration by the public opinion of their country of any proposals with which they might associate themselves. For we are throughout assuming that the conduct of foreign affairs and international relations must in the future no longer remain a close monopoly of a small governing and diplomatic caste, but must be brought under the control of public opinion operating through representative institutions. This new situation will have a vital bearing on the type of representatives best fitted for work upon the Council. Not lawyers or professional politicians are primarily wanted for this work, but able, broad-minded men of large personal experience of the people and the popular activities of their country, experience amplified by contact with the peoples and activities of other countries, men accustomed in large, free intercourse to test and assimilate new facts and valuations and to practise arts of mediation and of arrangement. Such men, drawn from the ranks of great employers, the labour movements, the Churches, the world of science, literature, or journalism, or from one or other of the learned professions, would form the proper personnel of such a Council. Endowed with a sufficient fixity of office and supplied with ample means, secretarial and other, and with the right of commanding expert assistance for special inquiries, this type of Council would form the best security for the peace of nations that the world could furnish.

If such a Council could be entrusted with the settlement of those large disturbing issues which in the past, under current methods of diplomacy, have ripened into dangerous quarrels, it would be an immeasurable gain. For the diplomatic method suffers from two fatal defects. In the first place, it is a discussion and a settlement, if settlement is attained, by avowed partisans. It is a test of skill and strength by which one party strives to get the better of the other, irrespective of the equities of the case. It is in effect a *modus operandi* of the Balance of Power. Though the players in this game make use of certain "rules" of international law, treaty engagements, or usages, their ultimate sanctions have no right relation to accepted law or justice, but are grounded in "reasons of State"—i.e. the supposed necessities or utilities of the nation they are said to represent. Though German statesmen and political philosophers have been more explicit in their avowal of this principle and perhaps more consistent in its practice, it has been the operative and determinant factor in all diplomacy. In a method where there is no provision for a disinterested valuation or decision, how can it be otherwise? For no appeals to international law or usage, even were these rules far more settled and authoritative than is actually the case, can dispense with an impartial tribunal for their application and interpretation. Moreover, as we have recognized, the issues which give rise to most danger are usually those which cannot in their nature be brought to any simple test of law or fact.

The second defect lies in the art of diplomacy itself and in the type of men who practise it in the Embassies and Foreign Offices of Europe. No one can study modern diplomacy in any of its critical phases without realizing the wide gulf which severs that art from the immense human interests it handles. First, consider the personnel of its operators, men drawn exclusively from the aristocracy and the wealthy governing class of each nation, men whose education and associations, interests, tastes, and habits of thought are those of a caste strongly entrenched in economic and social privileges and with few opportunities for gaining knowledge of or sympathy with the life of the general body of the nation.

Trace the life of these men in this country from the nursery to the Public School, the University, and through the preparatory stages of a diplomatic career, you will recognize how little they can be regarded as representative of the interests and well-being of their nation. Their initial outlook upon life is that of ease, security, and luxury, with that self-confidence and domination which are common to the class from which they spring. This temper of mind easily accords with a firm acceptance of ideas of the natural antagonism of the interests of nations. Drawn from this narrow section of society, they enter a calling strongly stamped with the traditions of an even less enlightened and more autocratically ordered past, in which the normal relations between States and Governments are envisaged in terms of suspicion, hostility, and jealousy. The conduct of diplomacy has always remained accommodated to this traditional attitude: its common phraseology, false-friendly, circumlocutory, and non-committal, full of duplicity and secret reserves, even using a bluff frankness as a choice method of deception, attests the *mala fides* of the art.

So long as the administration of our foreign policy remains exclusively in the hands of men selected from the one per cent. of families in a position to provide an independent income of at least £400 a year for a son entering the Diplomatic Service, the ideas, valuations, and methods of a sporting aristo-plutocracy of leisure will continue to mould our foreign relations. Even if the ablest and best-disposed members of this one per cent. were chosen for this most responsible work, the narrow basis of selection would sufficiently condemn the system. For though here and there an individual is able to liberate himself from the traditional outlook of his class and to cultivate popular sympathies, class sentiment must dominate the normal conduct of affairs.

Add to this the habitual secrecy in which all important negotiations and decisions are shrouded, and the absence even in the so-called democratic States of any real influence of the representative element upon the critical acts which may determine peace or war, and the full peril of the present secret bureaucratic policy is evident.[1]

[1] The Anglo-French Convention of 1904 affords an instructive example of duplicity in the respective statements of its "public" and its "secret" Articles. Articles I and II of the "Public Declaration" open thus:

This secret class diplomacy and its personnel are linked by a score of hidden influences and interests with the profession and the creed of militarism and with the powerful business interests which feed upon expenditure in armaments.

It comes, then, to this, that at present international relations are determined by a controlling personnel whose ideas, interests, sentiments, and modes of dealing are utterly unfitted to express the needs or will of the nations which they misrepresent, or to work towards the establishment of permanently peaceful relations between nations.

As a mode of dealing with grave and intricate matters involving deeply both the sentiments and the interests of peoples the diplomatic intercourse by interchange of letters, punctuated by overlapping telegrams, between persons residing in different capitals, often unacquainted with one another's personal qualities and necessarily precluded from all understanding of the nicer facts and feelings in the other's case, is a monument of ineptitude. Even if these same men, foreign ministers and ambassadors, whose misunderstandings, cross-purposes, and mutual suspicions brand

"His Britannic Majesty's Government declare that they have no intention of altering the political status of Egypt."

"The Government of the French Republic declare that they have no intention of altering the political status of Morocco."

The first of the secret Articles (as published by *Le Temps* in November 1911) reads as follows :—

"In the event of either Government finding itself constrained, by the force of circumstances, to modify the policy in respect to Egypt or Morocco, the engagements which they have undertaken towards each other in Articles IV, VI, and VII of the Declaration of to-day's date would remain intact."

every page of diplomatic correspondence, were set to "thresh out" the same matters round a table, it is certain that the more human relations then subsisting and the fuller facilities for probing the dark and doubtful topics would make pacific compromise far more possible. Indeed, if these unrepresentative types of men, with their false, antiquated conception of States and statecraft, could be superseded by groups of men representing the great popular interests and sentiments of their respective nations, the existing fears and risks of the failure of diplomacy would be very sensibly reduced. Though industrial conferences and Conciliation Boards do not give absolute security for the solution of industrial disputes, the personal contact helps to clear away much misunderstanding, and gives scope for the healing influences of humanity to express themselves.

How much more effective would be this method of conciliation if each party had to put its case before an International Council, the great majority of the members of which had no other interest than to discover the truth, conciliate the disputants, and keep the peace! Diplomacy is conducted in an atmosphere of estrangement, suspicion, or positive antagonism, and proceeds by intrigue, deceit, bluff, or bargaining to seek a settlement which it may fail to reach and which, if it is reached, expresses either an unsatisfying and unconvincing compromise or the triumph of one party, the failure of the other. Most settlements so reached are regarded as temporary expedients and leave trouble behind. International conciliation, conducted on the lines here proposed, would apply the skill, knowledge, and discretion of the Society of Nations to the disinterested task of finding "the best way out" and of urging its acceptance, with the fullest authority of informed public opinion. If nations could be got to perceive the supreme importance of this task and to appoint as their representatives upon the Council honest, able, and experienced men, capable of realizing the majesty of the position which they occupied as guardians of the public peace, the foundation of international government would be fairly laid.

CHAPTER VI

INTERNATIONAL FORCE

IT may easily be granted that after the experiences of this devastating war there will arise among the nations a disposition to give favourable consideration to the proposal here set forth of a Treaty by which the signatory Powers shall bind themselves to arbitrate all their arbitrable disputes and to submit all others to a process of Inquiry and Conciliation. But some will ask: "If we enter such an engagement with the full intention of accepting the awards of Arbitration and complying with the findings of the Council of Conciliation, what assurance have we that all our co-signatories will do the same? Unless you can show us that other nations more aggressive and less scrupulous than ourselves will feel, or can be made to feel, the binding force of their treaty obligations, the chief advantage of your League of Nations is not attained. For we shall still be compelled to maintain our separate national armaments, and to increase them if any neighbouring nation chooses to increase theirs." This objection, unless it can be met, is fatal. Can it be met? Let us first be clear as to what is lacking. We are assuming that a number of civilized States, including all or most of the Great Powers, are willing to sign a general treaty agreeing to submit any disputes which do not appear capable of settlement by ordinary diplomacy either to an international Court of Arbitration or to a Council of Inquiry and Conciliation.

In the matter of arbitrable issues they agree to submit their case and to accept and carry out the award of the Court. In the matter of non-arbitrable issues they also agree to submit their case and to take no military action during the process of inquiry. But they do not bind themselves to accept the findings of the Council of Conciliation or to adopt its recommendations.

Now, it is evident that if these processes are to become fully efficient for the preservation of peace, some common sanction of the Powers must support the pledge of the individual signatories. Here arise two important questions. What is the nature of that sanction? Is any definite concerted action of the signatory Powers required to make the sanction operative? If so, what international body should be invested with the necessary executive power? Otherwise no confidence will be established for these pacific modes of settlement. The mere substitution of a general agreement of Arbitration and Conciliation for the numerous particular agreements which exist already, even if its scope was extended so as to include every kind of dispute, would not, it may be urged, go far towards guaranteeing Europe against the possibility, or probability, of another war. For, under a sufficient strain of feeling or stress of circumstances, history shows that not Germany alone, or Russia, but every State has been willing to violate or to condone in others the violation of treaty obligations.[1] Even allowing for some recent quickening of the public conscience, it would be idle to pretend that the signature of such a treaty as is here described would give the requisite assurance for the fulfilment of its obligations under all conditions and by every signatory Power.

It may, indeed, be admitted that the co-operation of a large number of Governments in a solemn treaty of such momentous import would in itself strengthen the conscience of the world and evoke a power of international sentiment which most States would find it difficult to disregard. But is it credible that this moral and intellectual sanction for the fulfilment of the treaty obligations will suffice? This sufficiency, be it remembered, must be twofold. The moral sanction must be strong enough, not only to hold the least scrupulous of States to its pledges but to convince the most sceptical of States that it possesses such a power. Now, there have been pacifists, not a few, who in the past have been willing to rely upon the public opinion and conscience of the civilized world for a sufficient sanction. Nor has this faith in the power of public opinion been

[1] Recent instances are the breach of the Algeciras Act by France, with the backing of Great Britain, in 1911; the breach of the Berlin Treaty by Austria, with the backing of Germany, in the annexation of Bosnia-Herzegovina in 1908; the breach by Russia, with Great Britain's consent, of the stipulations of the Anglo-Russian Convention, securing the independence and integrity of Persia; and the recent breach by Japan of the Anglo-Japanese Treaty in relation to China.

confined to political idealists and humanitarians. So experienced a statesman as ex-President Taft, writing a few months before the outbreak of this war in support of a Court of Arbitral Justice for the authoritative settlement of " all justiciable controversies," thus states the issue : " But the query is made, 'How will judgments of such a Court be enforced? What will be the sanction for their execution?' I am very little concerned about that. After we have gotten the cases into Court and decided and the judgments embodied in a solemn declaration of a Court thus established, few nations will care to face the condemnation of international public opinion and disobey the judgment. When a judgment of that Court is defied it will be time enough to devise methods to prevent the recurrence of such an international breach of faith." [1]

Here, be it observed, Mr. Taft posits the existence of an international Court of Arbitral Justice, dealing exclusively with " justiciable " cases suitable for legal settlement. His proposals furnish no machinery for dealing with those more intricate and more inflammatory issues which, in accordance with our scheme, would come before the Council of Conciliation. Now, the terrible experience of this last year, with all its wreckage of treaty rights and international laws and conventions, has definitely weakened the current faith in the plighted word of nations and in the compelling or restraining force of international public opinion. Very few will now be found willing to trust the priceless cause of civilization to this moral guardianship alone, or to wait for " the recurrence of such

[1] "The United States and Peace," p. 150.

an international breach of faith " before devising a stronger guarantee.

Our League of Nations would certainly require its members, at the outset, to pledge themselves to bring concerted pressure, by armed force if necessary, upon any signatory Power which declined to fulfil its treaty obligations. Unless the force of international opinion in support of arbitral and conciliatory modes of settlement were strong enough to stand the strain of such a demand, both at times when Powers entered such a treaty and in emergencies when they might be called upon to enforce the terms, the proposal of a League is foredoomed to failure. For it is at least probable that cases would arise, at any rate in the early stages of the international arrangement, when some powerful State, acting either under sudden fierce resentment, or even by calculation of advantages, might seek to break away from its engagement, in order to work its will upon some other State with which it has a quarrel. If the League is to be effective, it must prepare for this contingency by the only possible method, that of bringing the united strength of all loyal members against the recalcitrant Power or Powers. It might, no doubt, be urged that this right of concerted action against a violator would be latent in the situation, and that, without any express obligation, the loyal signatory Powers might be expected to take such measures as they deemed suitable and necessary for the vindication of the treaty. The difficulties of arranging any method of joint action and of forming an executive to wield such power will dispose some persons to leave the ultimate enforcement of the treaty to some such *ad hoc* voluntary co-operation. This apparently is, or was, the view of Mr. Taft. But though the recent experience of arbitration indicates that States have in nearly every instance, however reluctantly, accepted the award of an Arbitration Court which went against their interests, we have no sufficient ground for holding that they would do so if there were included in the scope of arbitral reference issues of grave importance affecting "honour and vital interests," or that they would consent to refer to a Council of Conciliation the still more inflammatory matters which so often lead to war. In the existing rudimentary condition of the society of nations it would seem necessary to secure the integrity of the treaty by express provisions for its enforcement.

Now, within the scope of our arrangement for settling disputes there are five opportunities for recalcitrance.

The first two have reference to arbitrable issues. A nation might refuse to submit a case to Arbitration either because it denied the jurisdiction of the international Court or because it feared the result of Arbitration, or it might decline to accept or carry out an arbitral award which went against its interests. The proposed process of Inquiry and Conciliation affords three opportunities for recalcitrance. A State might refuse to submit to an Inquiry. It might resort to some act or preparation of hostility during the prescribed period. Or, finally, it might refuse to make a peaceful settlement after the Council had made its report.

If a breach of the public peace by any of these

acts is to be prevented, executive powers must be entrusted to some international body for the application either of preventive or punitive measures. It may be argued that since the prime purpose of the League is to prevent war, it would suffice if the signatory States undertook to take concerted action against any Power which, in defiance of its treaty obligations, actually opened hostilities against another Power. The breach of its undertaking to submit a case to Arbitration or Conciliation, or to accept the arbitral award, or to seek a settlement in accordance with the Council's findings, would not, on this hypothesis, oblige the Powers to take concerted action, unless and until such breach was followed by some overt act of armed hostility. It is, indeed, extremely probable that a League of Nations would be disposed, at any rate in the first instance, to adopt this restricted view of its executive duties. For it would be far easier to get States to consent to take concerted action against an actual aggressor resorting to war in defiance of his undertakings than to consent to do so in order to enforce the performance of these undertakings. It is, therefore, likely that the first agreement for common action against a breach of the international peace would take some such form as this: "All the Powers represented on the Court or Council to bind themselves by treaty, that, in case any Power resorts to hostilities against another, without first submitting its case to arbitration or to conciliation, or before the expiration of the prescribed period of delay involved in these processes, or in defiance of an arbitral award, they will support the Power so attacked by such concerted measures, diplomatic, economic, or forcible, as in their collective judgment are most effective and appropriate to the circumstances of the case."

A concerted action, however, confined to the single case of repressing hostilities undertaken by a State refusing Arbitration or Inquiry, could hardly be considered an adequate protection of the public peace. No means would have been provided either to redress an injury, other than war, inflicted by one State upon another, or to secure the peaceful settlement of any dispute, although the right and duty to do these very things are conferred upon it by the Treaty constituting the League. The powerful wrongdoer could with impunity refuse arbitration or inquiry and could continue his oppression and injustice, provided he took no step of actual hostility. A State, for instance, might deny protection to the life and property of members of a neighbouring State sojourning or travelling within its domains, or cut off its access to the sea and starve its trade, or assist a rebel party to prepare civil war within its borders. Nay, further, the injured State not merely would have no security or protection from the concert of the Powers, but it might have lost the right it formerly would have had of taking up arms on its own account against its oppressor. For such a step might constitute an act of formal aggression which it would be the business of the League to repress. Having regard to the necessity of building up an adequate authority for the international order, it would, I think, be recognized that the provisions of the

Treaty establishing means for the peaceful settlement of disputes must be covered by a fuller and a firmer sanction, involving a general obligation of the signatory Powers to take concerted action to secure the performance of all the treaty undertakings. The first Great Power which was permitted with impunity to refuse an order of the Council to meet a charge of oppression tendered by a weaker Power would strike a most damaging blow at the new fabric of internationalism. For it will be recognized that a League of Nations, confined in its executive aspect to the repression of hostilities when they occur, is inadequate to the elementary needs of the time. The Treaty constituting it gives it the duty of settling disputes between nations. It must have the power to perform this duty. Public opinion and moral authority will not in all cases suffice to induce nations to submit their case at the request of an International Council, to wait the result, and to accept the award. It would be idle to pretend that they will suffice. If nations are invited solemnly to bind themselves to arbitrate or to conciliate their quarrels and to accept the awards of an impartial international tribunal, is it too much to invite them to back their pledge to do these things by a further pledge to take part in com-compelling their co-signatories to fulfil their first pledge? I am told by some that the proposal to go so far as this is impracticable. Not enough States, it is urged, would consent to enter a League pledging themselves to take part in contingent wars which may involve no important national interests of their own, and where their sympathies may even lie with the recalcitrant Power upon the merits of the case. Other States, it is also urged, which might be willing to enter the Union if they thought that they could break away with impunity, provided the temptation were strong enough, would also be deterred by the more drastic remedies.

The objections are doubtless weighty. For the substance of our proposal involves a clear derogation of the rights of sovereignty as hitherto possessed by independent States. Each State is invited to cede the right of peace and war to an international body, upon which its own representatives will be in a small and permanent minority. Not only will it no longer have the right to make war *proprio motu*, but it will bind itself to make concerted war at the behest of this new international authority. This is the form of the invitation which, it is said, will seem intolerable to a proud and self-respecting State. But will it so seem when the substance of the proposal is considered? Will a peaceful nation whose arms are for defence, and which desires to make no forcible invasion upon the rights of other nations, suffer any real diminution of its own rights and powers? Its defence will be incomparably stronger than before, for all its territorial and other rights and possessions will be secured by the force of the other members of the League, in addition to its own. It is true that as a counterpoise it incurs the liability of having to take part in concerted action with other Powers against a treaty-breaking Power with which it may have been in friendly relations. To some critics this appears an insuperable obstacle. When it came to the point, we are asked, how could you expect that such a Power as Austria should fulfil her engagement to bring armed pressure upon Germany to compel the latter to carry out her treaty obligations? Or could you trust Russia to join in coercing a Balkan Federation, or Great Britain to take up arms against the United States in a quarrel which was not hers? But these objections seem to show some lack of imagination. For they are based on an assumption that all the motives which hitherto have drawn nations into particular offensive or defensive alliances and groups will remain as strong as before, and that, in fact, there must survive inside the great alliance here described those particular alliances with their disruptive influences which have defeated all previous attempts to maintain an effective Concert of Europe. Now, it would, of course, be foolish to ignore the certainty that for some time to come the amities and enmities of the present struggle will be represented in special associations and divisions which must weaken and imperil the larger international co-operation. But history teaches no clearer lesson than that of the facile dissolution of alliances which are not sustained by a powerful, evident, and continuous solidarity of interests. The nineteenth century was rife with the swift permutations and combinations of alliance between European States. The cement of a bloody war, conducted in alliance, is notoriously weak for binding nations. As the popular passions for war flare up swiftly into full intensity, so the animosities they leave behind die down much more rapidly than is expected. As with the economic so with the moral damages, even of the most destructive and exhausting wars, the rate of recovery exceeds all expectations. While the first feelings of triumph and of bitterness animate the victors and the vanquished, while the recent memories of the combat fill the mind and heart of the nations, while the direful consequences of the war are impressed upon every home and every industry, while the territorial changes and indemnities and other shocks to pride and pocket are still fresh, the reception even of the best devised schemes of international co-operation is likely to be tepid, and the maintenance of the old alliances may cross and hamper the new arrangements. But this early difficulty will rapidly diminish if the League of Nations can once be set upon a fairly stable footing and be given opportunity to assert its inherent virtues. For if the intelligence and faith of nations are strong enough once to establish it, the ambitions, the fears, and the suspicions, which are the spiritual nutriment of special alliances and groups, would wither and decay. So long as an ambitious, unscrupulous, aggressive State thinks that, by appeal to the special interests or fears of one or two neighbours, it can further its separate ends as a world-Power, it will continue to try to form secret or open alliances involving peril to the peace of the world. But if such a State found itself confronted by a numerous body of States (of which it and the particular States it sought to detach were also members) prepared to bring against it an overwhelming force of economic or military pressure, the design of forming such a special alliance or group would seem futile. Again, nothing can be more evident than that every special alliance is motived, as regards one or more members, not by aggressive intentions but by fear. Remove fear as a motive for alliances, and no alliances, involving peril to world-peace, would be established. Now, once grant the actual achievement of our League, with power to repress the depredations and oppressions of one Power upon another, the fear-motive would no longer bring nations into particular alliances. Neither for aggression nor for defence would these inner groupings any longer be valid. The psychological economy of the general as opposed to the particular alliance is complete. But this economy, it must be insisted, depends upon a clear acceptance of the necessity of an international executive vested with adequate powers to enforce the common will of nations.

The existence of such an international order would be itself the answer to the objection that nations could not in fact be relied upon to carry out their general treaty obligations by reason of the superior binding force which would attach to their special alliances with nations of kindred blood or interests. The *raison d'être* for these special alliances disappearing, they would be even shorter lived and less reliable than in the past. So long, however, as such special relations continue to exist between two nations, it would be a heavy strain upon the new international order to call upon one nation to take an active part in coercing another with which it had close ties, although the latter might have broken its obligations to the wider society of nations. The delicacy of such a situation would doubtless make it desirable that the International Executive should be permitted to exercise its discretion in exempting a nation so situated from this particular act of international service.

But to refuse such executive powers, upon the plea that certain States will either decline to enter the League if they are given, or will conspire to break their pledges and defy the consequences if they do enter, is tantamount to an admission of a lack of faith in the efficacy of the whole proposal as a safeguard of the public peace. Unless the desire for peace and the degree of confidence in the similar desire of other nations are strong enough in the proposed members of the League to induce them to undergo a self-denying ordinance in the employment of military and naval forces, and to consent to place these forces at the disposal of an International Executive for the preservation of world-peace, it seems unlikely that any treaty they may enter will possess enduring power.

The issue is of quite critical importance. This League of Nations must be regarded as the beginnings of an attempt to make a fresh advance in that evolution of human society which on its political side has grown from the primitive family or tribe to the modern national State or Empire. Indeed, its feasibility ultimately rests upon the fact that it evokes and posits no new or untried human powers, no new or untried political forms, but simply applies upon a larger scale those same powers and forms which have been successfully applied upon the smaller scale. It is the foundation-stone of a larger and more comprehensive human society, of which nations are the constituent members, made in the pattern of the smaller federations of which history has given so many instances.

The question of an Executive, invested with certain ultimate powers of safeguarding the fabric of constitutional and legal rights and obligations, has arisen in every form and scale of political association. Never and nowhere has it been found possible for a human association to dispense with the power to compel its members to observe its laws. Whenever this has been attempted it has failed. The present war, indeed, is the most tragically complete instance of the futility of expecting public law to operate and treaty obligations to be kept inviolate without an express and adequate and generally known provision for enforcing them. The reliance solely upon conscience, the inner sense of justice, and on public opinion, has never been found adequate for the preservation of the peace and the security of laws within the smaller structures of society. Is it reasonable to expect that this reliance can be adequate in the early stages of the large new association which brings together under common rules States hitherto acknowledging no clear moral obligations in their relations with one another?

There are, in effect, two separate and very diverse objections made to what is sometimes called the "Coercive Super-State." The first is that independent States will not so far surrender their sovereignty as to enter such a Super-State. With that objection I have already dealt. If it were valid, it would carry with it the despair of all attempts to secure a durable peace, and would throw nations back upon the necessity of seeking to maintain a precarious equipoise of nations and groups by mechanical Balances of Power.

The other objection comes, not from the hard, sceptical politician but from a certain type of idealist, who objects to the introduction of any coercive element of force into the control of international relations. He holds that the nations entering such a League can be trusted to fulfil their obligations : that the history of arbitration shows it : that the conscience and public opinion of the world are sufficient sanctions : and that these sanctions of moral force and reason are degraded and impaired by placing in the background a sanction of physical coercion. If force in the hands of a State is an evil, in the hands of a Super-State it is a greater evil. So runs the familiar argument. It is the argument of the moral force anarchist in State politics, in education, in penology, and generally in the arts of social conduct. There is nothing novel in its application here to international relations. History does not bear out any of its contentions. Nations cannot, any more than individuals, be trusted to fulfil all obligations. For, though arbitral awards have in nearly all cases been accepted, the number of arbitral cases involving vital interests and inflammatory questions has been very few, while recent violations of treaties and international laws prove that a moral sanction is often an inadequate safeguard. But the fundamental error is the assumption of an absolute antagonism between moral and physical force and the conviction that in any act of human conduct the latter can be dispensed with. No such antagonism exists. There is no display of moral force in any act of human conduct which does not make some use of physical force as its instrument. Such force is in itself no remedy, but it is a factor in every remedy which the intellect and conscience of men are able to devise. There is no purely moral suasion, no absolutely spiritual government. Civilization, the progress of humanity, no doubt, consists in the growing preponderance of moral and intellectual over the material factors in every art. But matter and force do not disappear. They continue to be essentials in every mode of human expression and achievement, individual or social, though they play a diminishing part. This is the tendency of progress, viz. to reduce the proportion of the physically coercive element in all control. But it cannot be dispensed with, or suddenly reduced, without disaster. Moreover, the idea that a large new extension of the scale of human co-operation, the beginning of an effective social life among nations, can be conducted on a higher moral plane than the social life within the most civilized of nations, dispensing with that element of coercion in government which no State dare dispense with, cannot claim serious consideration. The evil which the use of force involves varies, not with the amount of force but with the mode of its employment and the end to which it is applied. Force employed as the only means of breaking down a forcible obstacle to justice is not an evil but a good, provided it is not excessive. Nor can it be held that force is in itself degrading either to the user or the sufferer. So far as it is realized to be a necessary feature in the achievement of a just and reasonable end, it does not degrade. The degradation of war does not consist in the employment of physical force ; it consists in employing a maximum of physical force where a minimum would suffice, and in employing it for purely national purposes of the equity and utility of which there is no disinterested guarantee. The evil of war is that its result or settlement has no assured relation to reason or justice. In a world where reason and justice have been ingredients of growing magnitude in human affairs, war reverses the process. The gain of substituting the use of international for national force is twofold. In the first place, it reduces the magnitude of the rôle of force in the human economy. For, as I have shown, the indispensable condition of a general reduction of national armaments is this substitution of international for national employment of them. There would be much less force, and it would be far less frequently used. The second gain, however, is the determinant moral consideration. Assuming—and this is not in question—that the International Executive only employed force for the purpose of maintaining public order, and restraining a lawless nation from a lawless use of force, this would be a definitely moral use. The existence of this weapon does not degrade the nations who need no such restraint to make them keep their pledges. Paul expressed this truth with accuracy when he said that the law was not a terror to those who obeyed it, but only to the evildoer.

CHAPTER VII

THE ECONOMIC BOYCOTT

IN this discussion of an International Executive entrusted with powers to compel the fulfilment of treaty obligations, it must not be assumed that coercion can only be exercised by the employment of armed force. The boycott is a weapon which could be employed with paralysing power by a circle of nations upon an offender against the public law of the world. No nation to-day, least of all the great industrial and military Powers, is or can become socially and economically self-sufficient. It depends in countless ways upon intercourse with other nations. If all or most of these avenues of intercourse were stopped, it would soon be reduced to worse straits than those which Germany is now experiencing. If all diplomatic intercourse were withdrawn; if the international postal and telegraphic systems were closed to a public law-breaker; if all inter-State railway trains stopped at his frontiers; if no foreign ships entered his ports, and ships carrying his flag were excluded from every foreign port; if all coaling stations were closed to him; if no acts of sale or purchase were permitted to him in the outside world —if such a political and commercial boycott were seriously threatened, what country could long stand out against it? Nay, the far less rigorous measure of a financial boycott, the closure of all foreign exchanges to members of the outlaw State, the prohibition of all quotations on foreign Stock Exchanges, and of all dealings in stocks and shares, all discounting and acceptances of trade bills, all loans for public or private purposes, and all payments of moneys due—such a withdrawal of financial intercourse, if thoroughly applied and persisted in, would be likely to bring to its senses the least scrupulous of States. Assuming that the members of the League included all or most of the important commercial and financial nations, and that they could be relied upon to press energetically all or even a few of these forms of boycott, could any country long resist such pressure? Would not the threat of it and the knowledge that it could be used form a potent restraint upon the law-breaker? Even the single weapon of a complete postal and telegraphic boycott would have enormous efficiency were it rigorously applied. Every section of the industrial and commercial community would bring organized pressure upon its Government to withdraw from so intolerable a position and to return to its international allegiance. It may be said, Why is it that such a powerful weapon of such obvious efficacy has never been applied? The answer is that the conditions for its rapid and concerted application have never hitherto existed. For in order that it may be effective, a considerable number of nations must have previously undertaken to apply it simultaneously and by common action. And, what is more, each nation must have confidence in the *bona fides* of the intention of other nations to apply it. For the detailed application of the boycott, in most points, must of necessity remain in the hands of the several national Governments. Here comes the practical difficulty. Every boycott has a certain injurious rebound. It hits back the nation that applies it. The injury of suspended intercourse is, of course, not equal, otherwise the process would be futile. If the whole circle of A's neighbours boycott him, each suffers half the loss of his separate intercourse with A, but A suffers this loss multiplied by the number of his neighbours. Now if A's intercourse with all his neighbours is of equal magnitude, each of them can probably afford easily to bear the sacrifice involved in the boycott, trusting to the early effect of their action in bringing A to terms. But if one or two of A's neighbours are in much closer relations with A than the others, and if, as may be the case, they are getting more advantage from this intercourse than A, the risk or sacrifice they are called upon to undergo will be proportionately greater. They must bear the chief brunt of a policy in the adoption of which they have not the determinant voice.

Take, for example, the case of Germany. An all-round boycott applied to her would evidently cause more damaging reactions to Holland, Belgium, and Denmark than to any of the greater nations whose united voice might have determined its application. The injury to Holland, in particular, might in the first instance be almost as grave as that sustained by Germany, the supposed object of the boycott. It would evidently be necessary to make provision against this unequal incidence by devising a system of compensations or indemnity to meet the case of such a special injury or sacrifice.

A brief allusion to the other side of the objection will suffice, viz. the fact that any such boycott would be far less potent or immediate in its pressure against some nations than against others. While Great Britain would have to yield at once to the threat of such pressure, Russia, or even the United States, could stand out for a considerable time, and China might even regard the boycott as a blessing. But it is pretty evident that in the long run no civilized nation could endure such isolation, and that this weapon is one which the League might in certain cases advantageously employ.

Other aspects of the social-economic boycott raise other difficulties. While certain modes and paths of intercourse lie directly under the control of the Governments of the co-operating States, others belong to private enterprise. Though postal, railway, and telegraphic intercourse could be cut off easily by agreements between Governments, private trading could not so easily be stopped. It is not found a simple matter to stop all trading between members of nations actually at war when national sentiment sides strongly with the legal prohibition. It might be much more difficult to prevent all commercial intercourse for private gain when there was no special hostility between the two nations in question. But this is, after all, only a minor difficulty. Provided that the respective Governments were prepared to use their normal powers of control over the principal modes of communication and of transport, the potency of the boycott so established would appear exceedingly effective.

It involves, however, a risk which needs recognition. The extreme pressure of the boycott might lead to forcible reprisals on the part of the boycotted State which would, in fact, precipitate a war. Declaring what would be in effect a blockade by sea and land, it might be necessary for the League to patrol the seas in order to stop "illegal traffic," and to keep some force along the land frontiers for general purposes. A boycotted nation might, in the stress and anger of the case, begin hostilities against those of its neighbours who were most active in the operations of the boycott. In that event the economic boycott would have to be supported by armed pressure. This would also be the case where the breach of international law against which action was taken consisted, not in refusing to arbitrate or conciliate an issue but in an actual opening of hostilities. Such an act of war, directed necessarily against some one or more States, could not be met merely by a boycott. It would involve armed co-operation as well, the economic boycott forming an accompaniment.

There is another method of bringing financial pressure upon a law-breaking State which deserves consideration. It is put forward in the following terms by Mr. F. N. Keen in his able little book "The World in Alliance" [1]: "The States comprised in the international scheme might be

[1] P. 58. Published by Walter Southwood.

required to keep deposited with, or under the control of, the International Council sums of money, proportioned in some way to their relative populations or financial resources, which might be made available to answer international obligations, and an international bank might be organized, which would facilitate the giving of security by States to the International Council for the performance of their obligations and the enforcement of payments between one State and another (as well as probably assisting in the creation of an international currency and discharging other useful international functions)."

The organized concentration of international finance by the formation of an international bank is a line of action which might immensely strengthen that body of pacific forces the rising importance of which Mr. Norman Angell has so effectively expounded. It might consolidate to an almost incalculable degree the effective unity of the International League by placing under it the solid foundation of world-peace, while the power which such an institution would wield, either for purposes of fiscal or financial boycott, would be enormous.

But however highly we estimate the potentialities of the boycott as a valuable adjunct to the pressure of public opinion in compelling obedience to treaty obligations, it is idle to pretend that the confidence required to induce the chief nations to rely upon the due performance of these obligations by all their co-signatories will be possible without placing at their disposal, for use in the last resort, an adequate armed force to break the resistance of an armed law-breaking State. Somewhere behind international law there must be placed a power of international compulsion by arms. If that force were really adequate, it is probable that it would never be necessary to employ it for any purpose save that of repelling invasions or dangerous disorders on the part of outsiders. Its existence and the knowledge of its presence might suffice to restrain the aggressive or lawless tendencies which will survive in members of the League. But in the beginnings of the organization of international society it is at least possible, perhaps likely, that some dangerous outbreak of the old spirit of state-absolutism should occur, and that some arrogant or greedy Power, within the circle of the League, might endeavour to defy the public law.

For the States entering such a League will be of various grades of political development: some may enter with reluctance and rather because they fear to be left out than because they believe in or desire the success of the League. It is idle to imagine that a society starting with so little inner unity of status and of purpose can dispense entirely with the backing of physical force with which the most highly evolved of national societies has been unable to dispense.

What form, then, should the required international force take, and who should exercise it?

The proposal to endow some executive international body with the power of levying and maintaining a new land and sea force, superior to that of any Power or combination it may be called upon to meet, scarcely merits consideration. Apart from the hopelessness of getting the Powers to consent to set up a Super-State upon this basis, the mere suggestion of curing militarism by creating a large additional army and navy would be intolerable. Nor is it any more reasonable to expect the Powers to abandon their separate national forces, simply contributing their quota towards an international force under the permanent control of an International Executive. No such abandonment of sovereign power, no such complete confidence in the new internationalism, could for a long time to come be even contemplated. Each nation would insist upon retaining within its own territory and at its own disposal the forces necessary to preserve internal order and to meet at the outset any sudden attack made from outside. It is evident, in other words, that the forces required by the International League in the last resort, for the maintenance of public law and the repression of breaches of the treaty, must be composed of contingents drawn upon some agreed plan from the national forces and placed for the work in hand at the disposal of an international command. Such armed co-operation is, of course, not unknown. Several times within recent years concerted action has been taken by several European Powers, and though the Pekin expedition in 1900 cannot be regarded as a very favourable example, it illustrates the willingness of Powers to act together for some common end which seems to them of sufficient importance.[1] Is it

[1] The Dulcigno demonstration in 1880, the blockade of Crete in 1897, the demonstration at Antivari and the occupation of Scutari in 1913, are other instances, not to mention the great Alliance of Powers in the present war.

too much to expect that the nations entering the Confederation will realize with sufficient clearness the importance of preserving the integrity of their international agreement to be willing to entrust a permanent executive with the duty of commandeering the forces necessary to achieve this purpose when they may be required?

It will doubtless be objected that there is a world of difference between the occasional willingness of a group of Powers to take concerted action upon a particular occasion, for which each reserves full liberty of determination as to whether and to what extent it will co-operate, and the proposal before us. It is absurd, we shall be told, to expect that States bred in the sense of sovereignty and military pride will seriously entertain a proposal which may bring them into war in a quarrel not specifically theirs and compel them to furnish troops to serve under an international staff. But many events that have seemed as absurd are brought to pass. A few decades ago nothing would have seemed more absurd than to suppose that our nation would be willing to equip an Expeditionary Force of several million men to operate upon the Continent under the supreme control of a French General. Whether, in fact, such co-operation as we here desiderate is feasible at any early period will depend upon two factors: first, the realization on the part of Governments and peoples of the civilized world of the supreme importance of the issue at stake in this endeavour to lay a strong foundation for the society of nations; secondly, the diminution in the influence of militarism and navalism as factors in national life that is likely to occur if sufficient belief in the permanence and efficacy of the new arrangement is once secured. If nations can be brought to believe that national armies and navies are too dangerous toys to be entrusted to the indiscretion of national statesmen and generals, and are only safe if they are held in trust for the wider world community, this conviction will modify the surviving sentiments of national pride and national pugnacity and make it easier to accept the new international status. Moreover, if, as the first-fruits of the new order, a sensible reduction of national armaments can be achieved, this lessening of the part which armed force plays within each national economy will be attended by a corresponding increase in the willingness to place the reduced forces at the international disposal. For the root motive of the international policy is the desire of each nation to get a larger amount of security at a smaller cost than under the old order. Those, therefore, who confidently assert that States will not consent on any terms to entrust their national forces to an international command for the maintenance of the treaty obligations under the proposed scheme in effect simply assert the permanency of the reign of unreason in the relations between States.

For though the general agreement of States to submit their disagreements to processes of arbitration and conciliation with pledges to abide by the results would be a considerable advance towards better international relations, even if no sanction beyond the force of public opinion existed to enforce the fulfilment of the obligations, it would not suffice to establish such confidence in future peace as to secure any sensible and simultaneous reduction of armed preparations. No Government would consent to any weakening of its national forces so long as there was danger that some Power might repudiate its treaty obligations. This being the case, the burdens and the perilous influences of militarism and navalism would remain entrenched as strongly as before in the European system, advertising, by their very presence, the lack of faith in the efficacy of the new pacific arrangements. So long as these national armaments remained unchecked the old conception of State absolutism would still survive. There would still be danger of militarist Governments intriguing for aggression or defence in new groupings, and new efforts to tip the balance of armed power in their favour.

It is ultimately to the dread and despair of this alternative that I look for the motive-power to induce nations to make the abatements of national separatism necessary to establish an international society. Whether the end of this war will leave these motives sufficiently powerful to achieve this object will probably depend upon the degree of enlightenment among mankind at large upon the old ideas of States and statecraft.

CHAPTER VIII

THE INTERNATIONAL EXECUTIVE

WE are now brought to the consideration relating to the sort of International Executive to be entrusted with the powers required for the execution of international mandates.

Assuming that it is desirable for the nations constituting the League of Nations to take concerted measures to secure the fulfilment of treaty obligations, who shall organize and carry into effect these measures? There are several forms which this International Executive might take. The Court of Arbitration and the Committee of Conciliation, or one of them, might be entrusted with executive powers. Or the Concert of the Powers as constituted by Conferences of foreign ministers or their nominees might, as heretofore upon occasion, be recognized as the executive. Or, finally, some new representative international body might be endowed with the necessary powers.

Now, a very little consideration is required in order to rule out the first proposal, to give executive powers to the Arbitration and Conciliation bodies. Neither the type of man required for the work of Arbitration and Conciliation, nor the public status of this Court and Committee, will be suitable for the exercise of important executive powers. It is, we saw, desirable that the personnel of the Arbitration Court should consist chiefly of distinguished judges or jurists, men of high professional eminence in their respective countries, but not necessarily or normally endowed either with executive gifts or with wide personal influence among their countrymen. The functions of the Conciliation Committee, as we have sketched them, are of a different order, and the type of man required to perform them will have more of the practical experience which makes of him "a representative man." But in both cases it is desirable that the terms of appointment to the office be such as to secure the utmost independence of judgment and complete freedom from political pressure from the Government of the nation which is represented. For this purpose it is held proper that in both instances the term of office should be of considerable duration, so that the members of these bodies may be imbued as strongly as possible with the international points of view and sentiments befitting their office. But these very qualities for the performance of this judicial and conciliatory work are defects for the performance of the executive duties which we contemplate. For it is evidently of the utmost importance that an International Executive, not wielding full independent resources of its own but requiring to appeal to the constituent nations for co-operation, in order to enforce the common will against a breaker of the public peace, should consist of members who are in direct touch with the public sentiments of their countrymen, and whose judgments will be likely to have preponderant influence upon the public opinion of their nation. For to the Executive will be entrusted in extreme need the decision as to what coercive steps should be taken, economic or forcible, and by what nations and by what levies, in order to prevent a breach of the international treaty or to repress hostilities undertaken in defiance of the public law. It would be wrong to ignore the delicacy of such work or the importance of securing that the representatives empowered to commit their respective nations to such responsibilities be likely to secure the willing assent of these nations. On these two grounds, then, the integrity and independence of the arbitral and conciliation bodies, and the representative qualities required for the executive, it seems unwise to entrust the Court and the Committee with the enforcement of their awards or judgments. Indeed, as regards the Committee, there is the further difficulty that its reports, with suggestions and recommendations, cannot in the nature of the case have the same direct authority as is ascribed to the awards or judgments of the Arbitration Court. As proposals for conciliation they will necessarily carry in their form and tone the quality of advice and of persuasion rather than of express command. They cannot in all cases be taken as mandates which the executive authority should be entitled or required to enforce. At the same time, to refuse them all authority, and to leave it open to the several parties to disregard the recommendations, would weaken and might ruin the confidence of the nations in the most important instrument for securing the peace of the world.

It is quite evident that, whatever Executive is formed, its chief function will be to secure that nations shall not disregard the reports of the Committee, but that some agreement for pacific settlement along the lines of the Committee's recommendations, or otherwise, shall be carried into effect.

The performance of this duty would require that, if the Committee's recommendations were not such as to win the assent of the parties concerned, they should be taken into consideration by some other international body, vested with the power to frame out of them some definite policy which they were prepared to enforce.

What will be this third body, endowed with final judicial and executive powers? Two answers may be given to this question. It may be said that a Conference of Foreign Ministers or other accredited plenipotentiaries would be the natural body to exercise such final judgment and to take such concerted action as was demanded by the occasion.

The acknowledged claims for this method are two. First, that it involves no new structure, but relies upon a method which has frequently been employed, and which would almost automatically come into operation if no other arrangement were made to secure the enforcement of the treaty obligations, and to maintain the public peace when conciliation appeared likely to fail. Secondly, that the Foreign Ministers, representing their respective Governments, are the persons best entitled to claim to carry with them the influential public opinion of their countries, and are in the strongest position to bring about whatever concerted action, economic or forcible, is required to secure the public peace. Under these circumstances there would be a strong disposition on the part of the signatory Powers to such a treaty as we are considering to say nothing about enforcement of the treaty obligations or an International Executive, but to leave it to the course of events. This would imply, not that they had so much confidence in the faith and goodwill of all the signatories to the treaty of alliance that they deemed all express provisions for enforcement redundant, but that they shrank from the difficulty of securing agreement at the outset to any proposal to establish a formal International Executive. For this reason they would prefer to leave it open to the Foreign Ministers to deal with any case of infraction or evasion of treaty obligations according to the special circumstances. The elasticity of this method will be likely to commend itself to the gathering of statesmen and diplomatists in whose hands any arrangement for bettering the international relations after the war is likely to be left.

It will be defended as the most practical method of dealing with the situation.

But, regarded as a security for settling without war the dangerous issues which have been submitted to a Committee of Inquiry and Conciliation, or which some nation has refused to submit, the proposal has a fatal defect. It plunges the most critical and inflammatory issues back into that very atmosphere of diplomatic intercourse which history has shown to be so ill-adapted for pacific settlement. For if, as would be the case, all questions of enforcing the treaty obligations into which the nations had entered, and the still more delicate question of deciding what course to take when a nation refused the suggestions of the Council of Conciliation and proceeded to enforce its claims by hostilities, were left to a Conference of Foreign Ministers, calling themselves the Concert of the Powers, no presumption of successful arrangement is possible. For not merely would the members of this Conference approach the issue, as distinctively national representatives, with a minimum of the international spirit which may have governed the procedure of the Court and Council, but they would have the whole weight of tradition against the effective unity demanded for a strong common action. For the actual issue will be that of coercing a Power which admittedly has either broken an express treaty obligation, or has taken aggressive action against another signatory Power in defiance of the recommendations of the Council. Now the firm usage of these Conferences has been that the sovereign States represented thus cannot take action except by unanimous agreement. No majority of Powers has any claim to force the acceptance of its decision by a minority : such a demand would be resented as implying a cession of sovereignty. This means that one obdurate Power has always been able to nullify the Concert, or alternatively has been able to force a compromise that affords no satisfactory or permanent solution. Where, as would be the case in the circumstances we contemplate, the issue is the sharp one of bringing economic or military coercion to bear upon a Power represented in the actual conference, this tradition of concerted action, or of compromise, would be fatal. The distinctively national standpoint of the representatives, the habit of intrigue, the method of compromise, to say nothing of the actual presence of the law-breaker upon the judgment-seat, would make agreement upon any drastic coercion of a powerful State almost impossible.

Nor would it be possible to put the matter straight by proposing to shed the custom of unanimity which has conditioned action of the Concert in the past, and to introduce the practice of determination of the grave issues submitted to the Powers by a majority vote. In the first place, unless the Powers could be induced to set up and operate some sort of Constitution for their conduct of affairs in Conference, there would be nothing to bind a minority even of one to accept the will of a majority. Nor is there any likelihood that a Power or Powers, otherwise disposed either to break a treaty obligation or to refuse compliance to the recommendations of a Conciliation Council, would, in fact, accept as binding such a vote. There is, moreover, this further weakness inherent in a Conference of Powers. Whereas the Council of Conciliation gives weight in its Constitution and its work to the relative importance of nations, as indicated by their populousness and presumed strength, no such distinction is made, or could be made, at a Conference of Foreign Ministers. The difficulty is not perhaps so great in a Conference restricted to a few Powers, all of them "Great." But in a Conference where every State claims an equal voice, it would be possible that an issue might arise in which a majority decision was taken claiming to commit against their will to participation in some expensive economic boycott or military expedition a minority of States comprising some of the largest and strongest nations in the League. Though this division might not be probable, it would at least be possible, and the first time it occurred it would most likely strain the solidarity of the Conference to its breaking-point.

A Conference of Foreign Ministers cannot, therefore, seriously be regarded in the light of an International Executive to which could be submitted the important trust of securing the fulfilment of treaty obligations and the prevention of hostilities. The processes of Arbitration and of Conciliation, the results of which they were invited to uphold, should, so far as possible, embody the corporate wisdom and permanent welfare of the civilized society of nations. But this Executive would embody the resultant of the separate national pulls, determined by passing conceptions of expediency, and coloured by the personal sentiments and prepossessions of men bred in the usages of a narrowly national statecraft. There would be no natural accord between the spirits of the two processes. The internationalism would break down in practice on all critical occasions when the members of the League were called upon for corporate action.

What is the reason of this breakdown in our scheme? It is not that no Executive is provided for the International Government, but that there is a wide discrepancy between the representative character of the Council and that of the Conference of Powers which, in default of any other body, would be called upon to act as an Executive. The remedy is tolerably obvious. It is to provide an Executive which shall be as representative and as genuinely international as the bodies which perform the functions of arbitration, inquiry, and conciliation. This, of course, involves an action requiring great faith and courage, viz. the creation of a permanent International Council, elected by the constituent nations upon terms similar to those laid down for the Conciliation Committee and entrusted with those deliberative and executive functions which in a feeble and spasmodic way are wielded by the Conferences of Foreign Ministers meeting, usually too late, in times of crisis. Without such a representative body in permanent being, a deep sense of unreality will continue to attach to the Court of Arbitration and the Committees of Conciliation and to the treaty which shall claim to establish them as authoritative modes of settlement. For their authority will remain radically defective unless the same international will that creates them is also empowered to ensure the harvesting of the fruits they may bring forth. Why should not the nations which desire to secure peace and to support public law be assumed to be willing and capable of making such surrender of national individualism or absolute sovereignty as would undoubtedly be involved in setting up an authoritative elective Council with full powers to make and interpret international law and to regulate international relations in conformity with considerations of the general welfare? Why should not the Court of

Arbitration and the Committee of Conciliation be instruments of the International Council upon which would naturally devolve the duty of taking what measures were necessary to secure the acceptance of awards and proposals of settlement, and of exercising any economic or forcible pressure which might be necessary? We should then possess the rudiments of an international Government, which might be invested with such powers, legislative, judicial, and executive, as are essential to all government.

Before considering how far such an enlargement of our scheme is practicable, it will be well to remind readers that none of the smaller schemes appears to be effective in ensuring the maintenance of peace, the reduction of armaments, and the enforcement of public law, recognized as primary essentials of the required policy. An agreement upon reduction of armaments we saw to be utterly impracticable until the motives which hitherto have led to increasing and competing armaments were reversed, and no mere agreement by negotiation or treaty would reverse these motives. A League of Peace for mutual defence against aggression, even if it could be formed, would prove ineffective without some carefully contrived machinery for settling differences before they ripened towards hostility. But all such instruments of settlement, in order to inspire the necessary confidence, must in the last resort wield some authority to compel the obedience of reluctant parties. After careful consideration we rejected the claim that a purely moral sanction, the appeal to public opinion, would suffice to ensure acceptance of awards, and to inspire in all the Powers invited to come into the League full confidence that its awards would be carried into effect. Finally, we rejected the view that the Conciliation Committee could be entrusted with the necessary coercive powers, while the proposal to leave the several Powers the liberty they have always possessed to agree in Conference upon concerted action was shown to be a shirking of the issue, and to afford no reasonable likelihood of providing a solution in conformity with the international purpose which inspires the whole arrangement.

CHAPTER IX

AN INTERNATIONAL GOVERNMENT

PART I

Problems of Nationality

WE have approached the proposal of a representative International Council from the standpoint of the need of an authoritative Executive if the arrangements for pacific settlement of international differences are to work effectively. But this in itself would furnish an exceedingly defective statement of the case for an International Council. It presupposes a purely statical condition of international relations and of public law, and suggests that the co-operative action between nations could conveniently be confined to the stoppage of threatened or actual breaches of the established law. If every nation could be regarded as permanently fixed within agreed and definite territorial boundaries, with no needs, claims, or ambitions for political expansion or change of status; if all relations of trade, finance, or industrial development between the members of civilized States and those of backward countries could safely or possibly be left to private enterprise; if the changing fiscal policy, commercial and maritime laws, immigration policy, etc., of one nation did not vitally affect the welfare of other nations ; if such occurrences as the making of a Panama Canal, a revolution in China, the spread of bubonic plague or sleeping-sickness, involved no novel points of international conduct and evoked no new needs for international co-operation, our Council might be confined to the narrower task of securing the fulfilment of treaty obligations. But none of these assumptions is possible. We live in a world of change, and all political arrangements must be endowed with capacity of growth. No mechanical arrangement for the interpretation and enforcement of existing treaties, laws, and usages will be adequate to the security of peace. There must be power to alter past arrangements and to devise new laws, new usages, and new modes of co-operation. The words *rebus sic stantibus* are not only implicit in every treaty, but in all human arrangements whatsoever. These considerations make it clear that our machinery of pacific settlement and the work of our International Council cannot be purely judicial and executive. This, indeed, has already been admitted in effect by the larger duty of inquiry and conciliation assigned to the Conciliation Council. The functions of that body are differentiated from that of the Arbitration Court by the very fact that, whereas this latter is concerned with issues susceptible of determination by law or definite usage, the former is concerned with issues not so determinable. Its reports, based not upon the automatic application of existing rules, but upon broader principles of equity and welfare, in their reference to new "issues" or "situations" that have arisen, will, if they are effective, form the nucleus of new international legislation and usages. The report of a Conciliation Committee, with its recommendations, would not, indeed, as we have recognized, be held to have the same definite authority as belongs to an award of the Arbitral Tribunal, nor has it been proposed to enforce the acceptance of its recommendations. But none the less, if the body of international law is to grow, in order to keep pace with the changing facts of the time, it is these reports of Inquiry and Conciliation and the precedents they furnish which would rightly and naturally furnish the material and principles for this growth. But there must be some provision for adopting and adapting them to this end and of incorporating them into the body of international law. In other words, there must be a legislative as well as an executive power vested in our International Council. The report of a Conciliation Committee, whether it be concerned with a dispute between two nations, not justiciable in character, or with a deeper inquiry into some "situation" which has not yet ripened into a dispute, should be formally presented to the International Council, and should form material for its deliberation with a view to framing definite proposals. If the matter dealt with is a difference between two or more States, the International Council should, giving due consideration to the Report, formulate terms of settlement which should then have the same authority as an award of the Arbitration Tribunal, and should, if necessary, be enforced by the executive officers of the Council. In this way the fatal defect in the pacific machinery of settlement described in Chapter IV, which furnished no means of settlement in case a State refused the recommendations and, after waiting the prescribed period, proceeded to hostilities, would be remedied. A means would have been provided for stopping the last and most dangerous leak in the arrangements for securing a pacific settlement.

But such a settlement, formulated by the International Council, would in substance be a legislative rather than a judicial act.[1] It would take the recommendations of the Conciliation Committee as a basis for a rule of conduct, derived, not from existing law or usage, but from general principles of reason and justice as applied to a set of circumstances constituting the "case" or "situation." The reasoning upon which the "rule" was established would be regarded as valid for other similar cases, and would constitute an addition to the body of international law.

The same would apply to the results or reports of other inquiries of the Committee, directed not to definite disputes but to potentially dangerous situations in which, perhaps, the interests of several countries might be involved. An inquiry of this order, directed to the problem of the financial and industrial development of China or

[1] The natural tendency of any stable European concert to evolve a legislative function was illustrated by the action of the Congress of Vienna in making rules for the repression of the slave trade, for the free navigation of rivers, &c. It must, however, be borne in mind that this legislative function was but rudimentary, in that its decisions were only valid by the ratification of the several Governments.

Morocco, the problem of Asiatic immigration, or the maintenance of slavery under the title of indentured labour, would probably have led to decisions which would not merely remove the dangers that such issues contain when left to the several States to settle in accordance with their separate views of their several interests and claims, but would have evolved and established principles hereafter endowed with the force of public law.

A legislative function would thus attach itself to our International Council as a natural consequence and development of its judicial and executive functions, the judicial interpretation of the right and reason of particular concrete cases of conduct forming the basis of those general rules which constitute the body of public law.

If a really efficacious scheme for the establishment of peaceable relations is to be secured, it must assign to some duly accredited international body such powers, legislative as well as judicial and executive. Nor is there any reason to suppose that a Council so constituted would, or need, confine itself to the purely preventive functions hitherto ascribed to it. There is an immense and ever-growing field of constructive international co-operation which, though largely non-political, requires governmental aid and supervision. To the postal and telegraphic services, which are already regulated by international arrangements, add the rest of the vast and complex machinery of communications and transport by land and sea, the latter subject to many rules of international law and usage, the monetary and financial system, the intricate machinery of international commerce, the standardization of money, weights, and measures, the prevention of disease, human, animal, and vegetable, the spread of reliable information regarding crops, demands for labour, and trading opportunities. Many of these primarily utilitarian objects involve scientific and expert co-operation to which the concerted action of Governments is essential. For some of these tasks provision is already made for such co-operation, either by standing bureaux, as the International Postal Bureau at Berne, or by special Conferences or Congresses attended by officials of the several Governments concerned.

But an immensely enhanced economy would be given to this co-operation if its various branches could be gathered into a single centre and placed under a single international supervision and control. Many of these international affairs, at present conducted along the conflicting, uncertain, and shifting lines of special treaties or other agreements between separate pairs of Powers, might be reduced to a common, intelligible, and reliable system, with provisions for periodical revision and improvement, if they could be brought within the purview of the international authority.

The number and importance of matters comprising this field of positive internationalism must continually grow. Though many or most of them may be conducted mainly along the channels of privately arranged associations, there will be points where they touch and involve political arrangements, and where, on the one hand, friction may be avoided, on the other, positive advantages may be obtained by utilizing international political machinery. This is partially applicable to the commercial and financial processes of transport and communication by which men, goods, news, and money are moved about the world. This intercourse, so far as it is governed by the needs, wills, and ideas of individuals, constitutes a cosmopolitan rather than a distinctively international movement, but its regulations would naturally fall within the scope of our international government, which, in so far as it imbibed the spirit of this human intercourse, would itself become more cosmopolitan.

I have spoken of these large tasks of positive constructive co-operation by which nations might better develop and appropriate the natural and human resources of the earth, as distinguishable from the preventive work of pacifism which presses most urgently upon a world weary of war. But this difference between constructive and preventive work cannot ultimately be maintained. For a little reflection will suffice to show that the humbler schemes of safeguarding peace by processes of Arbitration and Conciliation are not likely to prove safe and satisfactory so long as nothing is done to cure the deep, underlying causes of the grievances, ambitions, and antagonisms of national or quasi-national interests which have always been the great disturbers of the peace. We have already recognized that it is not desirable always to wait until some difference or dispute has reached the danger-level before bringing to bear the instrument of international inquiry, and that Conciliation Committees might well seize time by the forelock in investigating situations which are potentially dangerous. But unless the International Council be empowered to deliberate upon the results of such inquiries, and to frame and carry into effect proposals for dealing with the potentially dangerous situations in time, our machinery of pacific settlement will remain very incomplete. Inquiry will not stay the process of events heading to a dangerous situation, which, in spite of Arbitration and Conciliation, may in the end lead to war. The strongest of all arguments in favour of an International Council, vested with the larger powers here claimed, is the urgent need of some impartial, authoritative power for settling on large constructive lines the two great related classes of problems which poison good international relations and make for breaches of the public peace. These are the problems of so-called nationality in relation to territory and government, and the economic problems involving international differences.

Taking the course of modern history, and particularly of the last century, we recognize to what a large extent wars have been consciously motived by the desire of subject nationalities to secure self-government and the control of the territories which they people, and by the desire of members of one nation to assist in liberating from subjection those of kindred race, language, or religion in a neighbouring country, or of effecting with them an independent political union upon a basis of common nationality. For our purpose it is not necessary to discuss the logic of such a term as "nationality," or to consider how far race, geography, language, literature, and religion constitute the likeness which inspires the sentiment of nationality. It is the community of sentiment and the powerful sympathy based on it that count for our consideration here. Where the feelings evoked are so strong that they are likely to endanger peace in an attempt to extort a territorial or governmental change, the International Council ought to be empowered to intervene, and to propose and carry into effect any changes of frontiers or of political allegiance which seem desirable. It is important to recognize that these questions cannot be settled once for all, but must continue to arise. Even if, as the result of the peace following this war, the map of Europe could be satisfactorily drawn along strict lines of nationality (a manifestly impossible supposition), there is no reasonable assurance that in twenty or fifty years' time these arrangements would continue to be satisfactory. Unequal growths of population in two adjoining districts of contiguous States, or of two diverse nationalities within the same State, the migrations from thicker to thinner populated countries, which will continually occur, and at more rapid pace with improved education and facilities of movement, will continually give rise to fresh demands for frontier readjustments along lines of "nationality" and for the self-government of large "nationalist" enclaves within the larger States. Great migrating populations from Russia or China that have settled in and developed large tracts of Corea or Mongolia may reasonably claim rights of self-government. Even within great States with democratic institutions similar problems might conceivably arise. If Russian or Scandinavian communities of large size in parts of North-West Canada, remote from the general development of Canadian life, built up what were in effect separate civilizations, preserving their own languages, religions, economic and social usages, they might create new nationalities which would not find adequate political expression within the limits of the local political institutions of Canada, but might crave a larger national autonomy. In this very manner the nationality of Canada itself and our other dominions has come into being. Where liberal political institutions thrive, such new internal growths of nationality are indeed less likely to cause trouble. But the world is large, and with the large scale of modern migrations it is reasonable to expect that demands for territorial readjustments upon grounds of nationality will continue to occur. Differences and disputes connected with such demands ought surely to form proper subjects for settlement by an International Council, informed by the accepted principle of all good government, the consent of the governed. There will be raised, of course, two important and obvious objections, one constitutional, the other practical. The former has reference to the desirability of assigning to an International Government a power to interfere with "the domestic affairs" of the respective nations. Such interference, it will be urged, speedily brought to ruin the Confederation of Europe framed a century ago. True, this interference was wielded in the interests of conservatism or reaction, and not of liberalism. But we are not now living in an era of accepted liberalism, and it may be urged that such States as Russia and Germany, which we should desire to include within our international arrangements, would certainly refuse to enter if so large a claim were made upon their rights of sovereignty. Even within the British Empire there remain large areas rife with the spirit of unsatisfied nationality. Should we consent to have the demands of India for self-government submitted to an International Council, which, perhaps, had just adjudicated on the claims of Finland and Albania?

Those who regard this war as primarily waged for the independence and the rights of smaller or weaker nationalities, and for whom the security of these rights is the first essential of a sound settlement, cannot evade the wider issue here raised. The reinstatement and indemnification of Belgium, the liberation from Austria and Germany of their Slav and other non-Germanic nationalities, and the adjustment of the conflicting territorial claims of the existing Balkan States, even if these objects can be satisfactorily attained, will be very far from meeting the full demands of European nationalism, to say nothing of the Asiatic nationalities, such as Persia and Armenia. Indeed, if the principle of nationality be once evoked as a basis of pacific internationalism, it will be impossible on any other pretext than that of conquest to defend its confinement to the cases of the non-Germanic provinces of the conquered Powers. Though the conditions of the Peace itself may look no farther than this restricted application of the doctrine, it will not be possible for any Conference taking the wider survey to ignore the pressure of the claims of Finland, Poland, and perhaps of Alsace-Lorraine to autonomy. Such a Conference, setting itself sincerely to seek security for the pacific future of Europe, would be compelled to urge a satisfactory solution of the other burning problems of nationality within the European system. If, further, any International Council, even of the less ambitious order, were entrusted with the right and duty of instituting inquiries into situations fraught with danger to the public peace, and of making recommendations for the solution of such difficulties, it would be compelled to take cognizance, not only of any existing unsettled claims of nationality but of the new claims which would emerge from processes of migration and peaceful penetration in various countries. A representative International Council endowed with governmental powers would then be placed in this dilemma: By basing itself upon a recognition of the territorial *status quo*, after the preliminary readjustments of the Peace, and refraining from all "interference" with the actual dominions of the sovereign signatory States, it would debar itself from any effective constitutional means of dealing with a class of issues which, from the passionate sympathy they evoke, will continue to endanger the public peace and to bring into disrepute the process of conciliation. For if no express right of adjusting the claims of nationalities is assigned to the International Council, the pacific recommendations of a Court of Conciliation are likely to be treated with contumely if they recommend the voluntary cession of territory upon grounds of nationality. A refusal of such powers would, therefore, leave untouched a fruitful source of international trouble. *Per contra,* if Sovereign Powers are invited to enter an international arrangement by which their territorial integrity might be impaired by a Council set in motion by a nationalist agitation within their borders and supported by the racial or religious sympathies of some powerful neighbour, it seems exceedingly unlikely that they would seriously entertain such a proposal.

This issue, of course, brings out most sharply the inherent difficulty of reconciling the two standpoints of national liberty and international government. Both are objects essential to the security and progress of civilization. So far as subject peoples are struggling for self-government, it seems evident that any scheme for securing peace must recognize this liberation as an indispensable condition of effective internationalism. Before nations can live together in society they must have their existence acknowledged and safely guaranteed. Nationhood must not be denied to any people who by racial, geographical, linguistic, religious affinities and by the feeling of community based on them, possess the essential character of nationality. This I take to be what Kant meant when in his great essay he laid down the principle, "The law of nations shall be founded on a federation of free States." This is indeed a hard saying, for it rules out, not only the subject nationality but the State which by the very fact of exercising dominion impairs its own freedom.

The real solution of the problem lies, however, in substituting, as far as possible, the word and the idea of autonomy, effective self-government, for the more confused and intransigeant idea of nationality which often craves for itself an absolutism of independence and of sovereignty that is inherently antagonistic to the needs of an international society. Autonomy is at once a more elastic and a more business-like conception. History shows that where the people of a district or locality are free to manage all those affairs which strongly interest them and closely affect their lives—e.g. trade and industry, religion, language, education—are not interfered with in their home-life, and are not unduly burdened with taxation, military service, and other demands of an outside or a central Government, the differences of race, language, and creed which may sever them from the other members of the State or Empire of which they are a part do not arouse deep discontent or any disturbing passion of "nationality." The French provinces of the Canadian Dominion, the Polish province of Galicia under Austrian rule, are striking instances of the efficacy of autonomy. It is not too much to say that the prospect of peaceful Internationalism depends more upon the substitution of the conception and the practice of autonomy for nationalism than upon any other change. For nationalism has always overstressed the separation and the sovereignty of nations, feeding those very sentiments of power and moral absolutism to which German political philosophy has given such unflinching expression.

Moreover, the concept of autonomy, with its elasticity, can alone furnish a solution for that terrible problem of the "rights of minorities" which is a thorn in the side of almost all nationalist movements. Local self-government is the greatest political healer, and if it be coupled with proportionate representation in districts where no local homogeneity is attainable, the practical demands for liberty and self-government are satisfied.

It is along these lines of effective autonomy that the international policy of the future should direct its pressure, rather than to the complete break-up of composite empires or kingdoms in order to erect new independent States upon a basis of nationalist sentiment. In the Peace treaty which concludes this war it is earnestly to be desired that the paramount importance of this consideration will be realized, and that no violent fusion of territory on grounds of nationality will take place for the establishment of independent buffer States, when guarantees for effective autonomy would be equally acceptable and far less dangerous for the peoples directly concerned, and would leave behind less bitterness in the conquered nations.

It is perhaps impossible to expect that any large number of independent States entering into such an international arrangement as we have premised would at the outset even consider a proposal to confer upon an International Council any general Power to intervene on behalf of oppressed or subject "nationalities" except in cases where the keen sympathy of some other nation of kindred blood, or with other close bonds of attachment, threatened a serious breach of the public peace. But an International Council, committed, by the initial policy of the Peace Congress from which it sprang, to the healing influence of autonomy and confirmed by experience in the efficacy of this principle, would probably find itself able to exercise a genuinely educative influence through the representatives of an oppressive Power for securing an effective remedy without the necessity of any direct authoritative intervention.

I do not, however, desire to beg any question as to the early possibility of getting "Sovereign Powers" to consent to invest an International Council with any sufficient powers to settle issues of nationality along the lines of autonomy. I have merely wished to indicate the desirability of building up, when it is possible, such international control, so as to prevent the birth and growth of one class of disputes which history shows to be most dangerous.

PART II

Problems of Economic Opportunity

STILL more urgent is the claim that an International Council shall obtain and exercise some sufficient power of considering and settling certain large questions of economic policy which bring modern nations into conflict. The growing co-operation of citizens belonging to different countries for all economic purposes, the interchange of goods, the use of the common ocean highways, the opening up of new markets, the development by capital of the resources of backward countries, the lending and borrowing of Governments and of private companies, the movements of labour from one country to another for the furtherance of world-industry —these mutually beneficial activities have given rise to much friction and antagonism between groups of interested persons in different nations who have been able to impose their ideas and interests upon the public policy of their Governments and sometimes to feed national animosities of a dangerous sort.

The growing dependence of modern civilized and thickly populated countries for the necessaries of life and industry, for commercial profits, and for gainful investments of capital upon free access to other countries, especially to countries differing from themselves in climate, natural resources, and degree of economic development, is of necessity a consideration of increasing weight in the foreign policy of to-day. Every active industrial or commercial nation is therefore fain to watch and guard its existing opportunities for foreign trade and investment, and to plan ahead for enlarged opportunities to meet the anticipated future needs of an expanding trade and a growing population. It views with fear, suspicion, and jealousy every attempt of a foreign country to curtail its liberty of access to other countries and its equal opportunities for advantageous trade or exploitation. The chief substance of the treaties, conventions, and agreements between modern nations in recent times has consisted in arrangements about commercial and financial opportunities, mostly in countries outside the acknowledged control of the negotiating parties. The real origins of most quarrels between such nations have related to tariffs, railway, banking, commercial, and financial operations in lands belonging to one or other of the parties, or in lands where some sphere of special interest was claimed. Egypt, Morocco, Persia, Asia Minor,

China, Congo, Mexico, are the most sensitive spots affecting international relations outside of Europe, testifying to the predominance of economic considerations in foreign policy. The stress laid upon such countries hinges in the last resort upon the need of "open doors" or upon the desire to close doors to other countries. These keenly felt desires to safeguard existing foreign markets for goods and capital, to obtain by diplomatic pressure or by force new markets, and in other cases to monopolize markets, have everywhere been the chief directing influences in foreign policy, the chief causes of competing armaments, and the permanent underlying menaces to peace.

The present war, when regard is had to the real directing pressure behind all diplomatic acts and superficial political ferments, is in the main a product of these economic antagonisms. This point of view is concisely and effectively expressed in a striking memorandum presented by the Reform Club of New York to President Wilson :—

> Consider the situation of the present belligerents.
>
> Servia wants a window on the sea, and is shut out by Austrian influence.
>
> Austria wants an outlet in the East, Constantinople or Salonica.
>
> Russia wants ice-free ports on the Baltic and Pacific, Constantinople, and a free outlet from the Black Sea into the Mediterranean.
>
> Germany claims to be hemmed in by a ring of steel, and needs the facilities of Antwerp and Rotterdam for her Rhine Valley commerce, security against being shut out from the East by commercial restrictions on the overland route, and freedom of the seas for her foreign commerce.
>
> England must receive uninterrupted supplies of food and raw materials, and her oversea communications must be maintained.

This is true also of France, Germany, Belgium, and other European countries.

Japan, like Germany, must have opportunity for her expanding population, industries, and commerce.

The foreign policies of the nations still at peace are also determined by trade relations. Our own country desires the open door in the East.

South and North American States and Scandinavia are already protesting against the war's interference with their ocean trade.

All nations that are not in possession of satisfactory harbours on the sea demand outlets, and cannot and ought not to be contented till they get them.

Nations desiring to extend their colonial enterprises entertain those ambitions for commercial reasons, either to possess markets from which they cannot be excluded, or to develop such markets for themselves and be able to exclude others from them when they so determine.

The generalization from these statements of fact is expressed in the formula, "The desire for commercial privilege and for freedom from commercial restraint is the primary cause of war."

Now, that the foreign policies of nations are, in fact, determined mainly by these commercial and financial considerations, and that the desire to secure economic privilege and to escape economic restraints is a chief cause of war, are indisputable propositions. So long as these motives are left free to work in the future as in the past there will be constant friction among the commercially developed nations, giving rise to dangerous quarrels that will strain, perhaps to the breaking-point, any arrangements for arbitration that may be made. An International Council could not be indifferent to this situation. What could it do? What ought it to be empowered to do? Before attempting an answer to this question, it may be well to distinguish between the real and the false antagonisms of economic interests between nations. Here a clear-cut distinction must be made between the two desires which the Reform Club statement asserts to be " the primary cause of war." The desire for commercial privilege is not on all fours with the desire for freedom from commercial restraint, or " the open door." Commercial privilege, whether expressed in tariffs or bounties, in concessions or monopolies, or in " close " colonies, protectorates, and " spheres of influence," is in no true sense a " national " interest, nor is it an expression of a " national " desire. These acts of policy result, partly from the voluntary adoption by unenlightened statesmen of false notions of national economy, but mainly from the pressure of particular commercial, manufacturing, or financial interests within each nation. This usurpation of foreign policy by private interests usually inflicts two commercial injuries upon the nation it pretends to serve. So far as it operates by tariffs, bounties, or " monopolies," it injures the total productive powers of the nation by disposing them in an uneconomical manner, which comes home in diminished powers of national consumption. So far as it operates by a strong foreign and colonial policy, in order to win privilege and profits for special groups or interests within the nation, it imposes enormous burdens of taxation for the maintenance of those armed forces and the conduct of the wars and expeditions which are entailed by such a policy. Even in cases where this policy opens up new areas of profitable trade, not only for special business interests, but for the larger body of a national trade, a faithful statement of the *per contra* account, in the shape of direct and indirect public expenditure, would usually show a large net deficit from the standpoint of the nation. In a word, Protection, Imperialism, and a "spirited foreign policy" do not pay a nation. Economic privileges are not legitimate objects of national desire, and Governments intelligently sensitive to national interests will not seek such privileges.

On the other hand, equality of commercial and financial opportunities in the shape of freedom of access by sea and land to foreign countries, freedom of trade with the inhabitants of such countries, and equal opportunities for capital and labour to take part in the economic development of such countries are advantages, not only for the particular interests directly engaged in such intercourse but for the nation as a whole. So far, therefore, as the desire "for freedom from commercial restraint" is a cause of war, we are confronted with a real grievance affecting the interests of a nation, not only of a group. The fears of a nation lest their commerce and manufactures should be injured by protective tariffs or by "close colonization" on the part of other nations have a real foundation. Such a policy may even endanger supplies of foods and other necessaries upon which nations have grown to rely. At any rate, their manufacturing and commercial progress is liable to be seriously hampered if other advanced nations close against their goods, not only their own markets but those of their colonies and protectorates. Reflection will show that the aggressive factor of German militarism was able by the recent course of events to work powerfully upon the fears of the business classes of the country lest German trade should be subjected to this strangling process, and that without such appeals it is unlikely that the nation could have been worked up to the temper required for war. The close Protectionism of the French colonial system, recently and in defiance of treaty rights extended to Morocco, the counter-working of Great Britain and France against the efforts of Germany to secure "places in the sun," and, lastly and chiefly, the conviction that Great Britain was likely soon to abandon the Free Trade hitherto practised throughout her Empire were important factors in the causation of the war.[1]

[1] A well-known Belgian economist gives the following account of this economic *motif* in German policy :—

"L'Empire d'Allemagne a une population constamment croissante (à raison de près d'un million par année) de près de 70 millions d'habitants dont les industries et le commerce ne sont assurés que de leur marché intérieur et de marchés coloniaux relativement insignifiants. Le territoire de l'empire allemand est exactement dix fois moindre que celui de l'empire britannique et ne sera susceptible d'être occupé dans l'avenir que par un nombre supplémentaire fort limité d'habitants et de consommateurs des produits allemands. Quant à tous ses autres marchés, le peuple allemand, dont les besoins, les désirs et les moyens d'expansion extérieure sont des plus considérables—et entièrement légitimes—se trouve, il faut le reconnaître, dans une situation précaire.

"L'esprit protectionniste place les relations des peuples sous un régime de simple tolérance, toujours susceptible de se transformer en parfaite intolérance, celle-ci pouvant s'appliquer alors aux hommes comme aux produits. Ce n'est certes pas l'un des moindres inconvénients du protectionnisme que l'instabilité et l'insécurité générales qui en résultent—pour ceux qui le prati-

Disputes arising from these economic causes are even deeper seated and more dangerous than those connected with the claims of nationality and autonomy. Indeed, political autonomy is shorn of most of its value unless it is accompanied by a large measure of economic liberty as regards commercial relations with the outside world. The case of Servia, liable at any moment to be denied access to the sea, or to be cut off by Austria from her chief land markets, is a case in point. Or once again, would the autonomy of such a country as Hungary, Bohemia, or Poland, however valid its political guarantees, satisfy the legitimate aspirations of its population if high tariff-walls encompassed it on every frontier? Such instances make it evident that no settlement of "the map of Europe" on lines of nationality can suffice to establish peace. The effective liberty of every people demands freedom of commercial

quent, comme pour ceux contre lesquels il est dirigé. Protectionniste, l'Allemagne cause aux autres et subit, elle-même, ces inconvénients. La Russie n'annonçait-elle pas, en juillet dernier, qu'elle avait en vue de profondes modifications du traité de commerce russo-allemand échéant en 1916? La France ne se disposait-elle pas à se procurer par un nouvel accroissement de ses droits douaniers les ressources nécessaires à l'application de la 'loi de trois ans'? Les citoyens des Etats-Unis, sont-ils, en majorité assurée, convertis à la politique de la liberté des importations? Et faut-il exclure des possibilités que l'Angleterre compte dans 10 ou 15 années une majorité d'électeurs favorables à un projet de tariff-reform et à la constitution d'un grand empire économique fermé?

"Que la situation économique de l'Allemagne soit précaire, en ce qui concerne ses débouchés étrangers, ne peut pas être contesté." ("Un Autre Aspect de la Question Européenne et une Solution," par Henri Lambert.)

intercourse with other peoples. A refusal or a hindrance of such intercourse deprives a people of its fair share of the common fruits of the earth, and deprives the other peoples of the world of any special fruits which it is able to contribute to the common stock.

If any international Government existed, representing the commonwealth of nations, it would seek to remove all commercial restrictions which impair the freedom of economic intercourse between nations.

These restrictions are placed by the Reform Club Memorandum under the four following categories :—

First. There is the restriction of tariffs imposed by nations.

Second. There are restrictions upon the best uses of International commerce, of the terminal and land transfer facilities of the great trade routes and seaports of the world. A few such ports command entrance to and exit from vast continental hinterlands. It is vital to these interior regions that their natural communications with the outside world should be kept widely open, and this is equally vital to the rest of the world. Obstructive control of such ports and routes to the detriment of the world's commerce cannot and should not be tolerated by States whose interests are adversely affected. But routes and ports are needed for use, not government; and port rivalries constantly tend towards offering the best and equal facilities to all. The swelling tides of commerce are clearing their own channels, and mutual interests will more and more prompt the States through which the principal trade routes pass to facilitate the movement of commerce.

Third. There are restrictions upon opportunities to trade with territories ruled as colonies or being exploited within spheres of influence. This is what now remains of the old mercantile system which flourished before our revolutionary war, and which has been weakening ever since. Great Britain claims no preference for herself in her colonies. Other States have been less liberal. The fear of such restrictions being applied against them is to-day the main motive for a policy of colonial oversea possessions. If industrial States could be assured of the application of the open-door policy, no State would envy another its colonies. Colonies should be the world's.

Fourth. There are restrictions in the free use of the sea. Unlike land routes, ocean routes are offered practically without cost to all, whithersoever the sea runs. Over these, however, until modern times commerce has been subject to pillage by regular warships as well as by pirates. The claims of commerce have been more slowly recognized on the sea than on the land; and, to an extent now unthinkable on land, warring States still feel free to interfere with neutral traders."

Now what could an International Council do for the removal of such injurious and provocative restrictions?

As regards the tariffs and other methods of Protectionism, they could exercise no direct control. For tariffs and other Protective instruments, however injurious to other nations in their effect and their intention, belong to the financial systems of the several nations which employ them as modes of regulation of national trade and of national revenue. Their removal could not be effected by such an international Government as is here contemplated. It must be left to the common sense and goodwill of the several nations to expose the delusions and to overcome the selfish private interests which impose so injurious a public policy upon their respective Governments. But the free deliberations of the International Council would be a powerful educative influence for the exposure of the fallacies and the injuries of Protectionism, and would furnish better facilities for mutual arrangements and the avoidance of tariff wars. As the general benefits of international co-operation gained increasing recognition among statesmen and peoples, it might be expected that the spurious nationalism which finds its commercial expression in Protection would continually weaken, and that tariffs, so far as they survived, would be more and more "for revenue only."

Direct action by mutual arrangement for the removal of the other classes of restriction would, however, fall within the scope of an International Council that was empowered to deal with the removal of the roots of war and the conditions of effective international co-operation.

Equality of opportunity for commerce, for investment of capital, and for participation in the development of the world's resources, is the first condition for the progress of national civilization in the world. In the fruits of such progress every people should get its share, and the co-operation in this common task is the surest bond of peace among nations. Cobden was not mistaken in regarding Free Trade as a great peacemaker. But he could not foresee two counteracting influences due to mal-distribution of economic and political power among the respective classes in the industrial nations. The distribution of the immensely growing product of modern industry between capital and labour has been such as to place at the disposal of capitalist employers a producing power which continually tends to outrun the effective demand for the goods which it is able to produce. In other words, national production of such goods tends to exceed national consumption, which is kept down by the inadequate share possessed by labour in the product of industry. This condition of affairs has driven competing manufacturers and traders to use every means of finding or of forcing foreign markets, in order to dispose of the surplus over the demands of home markets. This struggle for overseas markets has been notoriously a growing factor in foreign policy and a growing source of international friction.

Another factor of increasing importance in the recent conflict of nations has been the competition between groups of financiers and concessionaires, organized upon a "national" basis, to obtain exclusive or preferential control in the undeveloped countries for the profitable use of exported capital. Closely related to commercial competition, this competition for lucrative investments has played an even greater part in producing dangerous international situations.[1] For these financial and commercial interests have sought to use the political and the forcible resources of their respective Governments to enable them to obtain the concessions and other privileges they require for the security and profitable application of their capital. The control of foreign policy thus wielded has been fraught with two perils to world-peace. It has brought the Governments of the competing financial groups into constant friction, and it has been the most fruitful direct source of expeditionary forces and territorial aggressions in the coveted areas. As the struggle for lucrative over-

[1] See Mr. H. N. Brailsford's important book, "The War of Steel and Gold" (G. Bell & Sons).

seas investments has come to occupy a more important part than the struggle for ordinary markets, the economic oppositions between European Governments have become more and more the determinant factors in foreign policy, and in the competition of armaments, upon which Governments rely to support and to achieve the aims their economic masters impose upon them.[1]

Any International Council entrusted with the duty of preventing and not merely of settling disputes would be obliged to grapple with these thorny issues. Asia, Africa, and South America still contain huge undeveloped areas of economic exploitation, which to keen-witted business men are "spheres of legitimate aspiration" to be realized by the assistance of their respective Foreign Offices with the finances and the forces of the State at their disposal. What should be the principles of international policy in the "development" of the resources of backward countries? Some constructive policy must be applied. A mere doctrine of "hands off," urged sometimes by Socialists in their capacity of anti-capitalists, sometimes by extreme nationalists, concerned to assert the absolute ownership of every country by its inhabitants, is not seriously defensible, on grounds either of ethics or of practical politics. The

[1] This account of the influence of financial competition must not be understood as an attack upon the export of capital. The free movement of capital, as of goods and men from one country in the world to another, is in its normal operation a pacific force, binding the different creditor and debtor nations together by mutual advantages. Only when national groups of capitalists employ political weapons to gain their private ends does the export of capital become a source of danger.

occupiers of a land containing rich resources which can be developed for the benefit of mankind have no "right" to withhold them. If they cannot or do not desire to develop them themselves, they cannot properly resent the claim of outsiders to come in and do this work. The question is, What are the governing principles which should regulate such justifiable interference? Two vices are disclosed in the actual history of such interferences. Upon the first—viz. the jealousy and friction created between the dominant economic groups and the Governments of competing States—I have already dwelt. The second is the economic injustice and oppression commonly inflicted by the "civilized" exploiters upon the "natives" of these areas of exploitation, and the political injustice and oppression often inflicted by the Governments of the exploiters through the assertion of political dominion. If the right of outside interference is based upon the claim to develop for the general good the otherwise wasted resources of a foreign country, only so much interference, economic and political, as is required to achieve this end is *primâ facie* justified. This common right of nations ought not to be permitted to be made a pretext and an opportunity either for a policy of plunder and servitude by groups of privileged profiteers, or for a policy of Imperial aggrandizement by their Government.

Now, an International Council, concerned primarily to keep the peace and to substitute co-operative for competitive action on the part of its constituent nations, might proceed along either of two lines. It might pursue a policy of political and economic "partition," as in the great African deal of 1885, assigning to its several members separate spheres of economic interest for exploitation, and leaving to them the right to exclude the capitalists and traders of other civilized nations from concessions or trade within their sphere. This would be the worst international arrangement, both from the political and the economic standpoint. For there could be no security that a "fair" partition could be made, preventing jealousy and affording durable satisfaction; while the stimulus thus given to Protection and to economic privilege would both impede the best development of the exploited countries and foster commercial disputes.

Or a "partition" might be made which, having regard to the special political and economic interests of particular nations by virtue of accessibility or established connections, would acknowledge a special right of intervention and even of political control, but with an express agreement to maintain an open door and equality of opportunity for the capital and trade of other nations. This principle has been embodied, more or less completely, in some recent treaties[1] between several Powers, though the lack of adequate guarantees for the faithful performance of the undertakings has made such arrangements exceedingly precarious.

If, however, a standing International Council could be empowered to negotiate such partitions, with periodic arrangements for revision, the dangerous collisions of economic interests which

[1] E.g. the Algeçiras Treaty.

have underlain the policy of political and economic expansion in the past might be reduced to a minimum. For the attainment of the "open door" would not only stop the pressure which competing groups have hitherto placed upon their respective Foreign Offices: it would directly promote the substitution of international for purely national groups and syndicates, giving free play to the genuinely co-operative tendency of modern finance. If powerful trading and financial groups within each country were no longer goading, bribing, or cajoling their respective Governments to threaten and outwit one another in obtaining economic privileges for their respective nationals, the chief modern cause of war would disappear. Although the established interests and modes of public finance in the parts of the world already allotted might make the retrospective application of "equality of economic opportunity" slow and difficult, it ought not to be impossible to neutralize those areas which have not yet passed into exclusive national preserves. The example of Great Britain in her Crown colonies and protectorates would serve to give a lead along this path to a sane world-policy.

There is, however, one important problem of economic opportunity for which no early solution could be found by any International Council, however representative. The utilization of the economic resources of the world for the benefit of the world demands the open door, not only for trade and for capital but for labour. If world policy were to be measured merely in terms of the maximation of material wealth, it is pretty clear that the principle of *laissez faire, laissez aller* would demand the removal of all restrictions upon migration, in order that labour might flow as easily and rapidly as possible to the area where higher wages would denote greater productivity. Indeed, such a mobility of labour is closely linked with the mobility of capital that appertains to sound internationalism. Capital cannot operate without labour, and though it may sometimes find a suitable supply of labour on the spot, it often needs to draw it from elsewhere. Now though facilities of modern transport have given immensely increased mobility to labour, certain obstinate and tightening restrictions are placed by many nations upon the direction, character, and pace of this flow. The great natural areas of emigration are countries of congested population, living upon low standards of comfort, but capable of hard or skilful work in "new" countries. The continent of Asia is a rich reservoir of such labour. China and India contain huge surpluses of population capable of common service in America, Australasia, and South Africa, and willing to undertake this service. But the difficulty of procuring the general assent of civilized nations to "an open door" for Asiatic labour would, of course, be insuperable, and no International Council could undertake the task with any prospect of success. For restraints upon such free immigration do not rest merely or mainly upon economic delusions, gradually to be dissipated by saner and more scientific views of national policy, as is the case with the restrictions on freedom of commerce which the same Governments frequently apply. They are rooted more deeply in a broader social-economic policy of those nations. While, therefore, it would be possible that the educative intercourse of international government and the improved facilities of international arrangements might gradually bring about reductions of protective tariffs, it could not be expected that a similar effect could be produced upon the immigration laws and other disqualifications which check the free entrance and settlement of "coloured" peoples in many countries governed by white peoples. The claims of the more prolific and congested coloured races for equal opportunities in the development of under-peopled countries by their labour will continue to present problems for which a Council representing "civilized" Powers can find no early solution. It is, however, possible that some common policy adopted by such a Council might mitigate the resentment felt by members of such civilized countries as China, India, and Japan, by securing to the yellow, black, and brown races sufficient areas of free migration and exploitation in the tropics to relieve, or at any rate postpone, the graver issues of race antagonism which may threaten the future peace of the world.

There remains one difficulty inherent in the type of international Government we are considering. The dealings of civilized and powerful States with uncivilized and weaker peoples have always been selfish and commonly oppressive. May not a Council, representing all the civilized and powerful States, be similarly selfish and oppressive in its attitude? Its power to be oppressive with safety and impunity will be far greater than that possessed by any "imperialistic" nation in the past. Could the white nations of the earth thus banded together be entrusted with the fate of their coloured fellow-beings? What security would the latter have that they would not be kept in a state of political serfdom, called by those who impose it "good government," in order that the natural and human resources of their country may be utilized for the good of a world to which they are outsiders? Indeed, this same objection may be raised on behalf of civilized peoples which either are not included in the international company or which, being members, may yet find that the control of international affairs is actually wielded by an inner circle of "Great Powers" imposing its corporate will unjustly and oppressively upon the smaller nations. In other words, it is difficult to pre-figure an international Government that can be trusted not to abuse the tutelage over "lower" or "backward" peoples, and not to preserve in its demeanour and operations some of the pride of power and selfishness which the official representatives of great States have always exhibited in their dealings with small States. The problem in the two cases is not, indeed, the same; but the successful solution, so far as it is attainable, involves the application of the same principle. The tendency of powerful States to domineer over weaker States within the international society is in substance the same issue as is raised by the class struggle within a State. It can only be remedied by a more intelligent co-operation of the weaker members on the one hand, and by an increasing sense of human solidarity upon the other. A disposition of a Power, or group of Powers, to attempt to use the international policy for the furtherance of its particular interests at the expense of others is likely enough to manifest itself in the early stages of the evolution of a society of nations. It may even lead to a temporary break-up or collapse of the experiment. But the necessities of the situation will compel attempts at reconstruction, perhaps on a better and fuller basis of representation. The faults and failures of international conduct, the oppression which international society may seek to exercise over the outside world are necessary defects of its quality, only to be remedied, as defects of individual and national character are remedied, by the expensive process of experience. There can be no denial of the dangers of an abuse of international power. But the more completely international it becomes the less frequent and less injurious will these abuses be. Every extension of the area of effective internationalism, every growth of the international mind by co-operative practice, will diminish the danger of an undue preponderance of power remaining in the hands of a great State, or a group of States, inclined to exercise unjust dominion or oppressive exploitation over weaker members of the social union or over unrepresented peoples.

If, then, peaceable relations between nations are to be secured by conferring upon some Council, Congress, or other representative body, an adequate power, not merely to settle dangerous disputes but to prevent them from arising, this preventive policy, in order to be really effective, requires us to envisage a form of international control or government endowed with considerable executive and legislative functions. It must be competent to frame rules or laws of general validity for dealing with the new needs and new situations which will arise in history from the new contacts, new pressures, and new conflicts of interest between nations or their Governments. The legislative and executive activities of such an international Government cannot, therefore, be narrowly confined to some simple methods of preventing war and regulating armaments. In order properly to accomplish their conservative task of keeping order in a changing world they must be progressive. In this chapter we have chiefly dwelt upon what is properly regarded as the legislative aspect of this work. The executive work we have considered chiefly from the standpoint of the powers that must be exercised internationally, if the arrangements for settling disputes by arbitral and legal methods are to be adequately guaranteed. This approach, however, has given a very partial significance to the executive powers which such a Council or Congress would have to wield. By stressing the question of guarantees it has ignored the international Civil Services required for carrying on the ordinary work of the Council and the Courts and for administering their rules and judgments. Yet this official work and the finance which it involves will be of great and continually increasing importance, establishing habits and rules of orderly co-operation and adjustment which in themselves will furnish a valuable educational support to internationalism.

If, further, we take into account the growth and transfer to the Council of those numerous forms of positive international co-operation, designed not primarily for the preservation of peace but for the pursuance of the common welfare of nations, we perceive that an international Government, once fairly established, will exhibit natural powers of growth for legislative and administrative purposes to which no close limits can be set. Just as within a federal State, or a federation of States, the central power continually receives new accessions, by virtue of the widening needs and interests of the members of this national society, so the actual growth of international contacts and communications will have a similar effect in feeding the organs of international government. In this process, however, there is nothing really inimical to the survival and strength of nationalism. Effective growth of local self-government is consistent with a continual positive enlargement of the powers of the central Government. For in a progressive community there is a constant enlargement of the aggregate of government, and the functions thrown on to the centre are, or may be, fully compensated by the orderly devolution of other powers from the centre, as well as by the growth of fresh functions of local origin. This same economy in the relations between local and central Governments would be exhibited upon the larger scale if the federal principle were once fruitfully applied to a society of nations.

CHAPTER X

THE SOCIAL CONTRACT OF NATIONS

It is likely that some readers will have been growing impatient during the process of developing an international design so far-reaching as that indicated in our last chapter. " It will be difficult enough," they will say, " to get the princes and statesmen of Europe to look with favour upon any scheme for the pacific settlement of all matters of dispute. But to invite them even to consider your fuller scheme of international government, not only is futile in itself but is calculated to damage the chance of the more modest proposals." To reply, as we might, that the more ambitious architecture of our scheme has grown by the natural and logical process of remedying the proved and admitted defects of the simpler proposals will hardly satisfy our critics. It will, therefore, be better frankly to admit that to ministers and diplomatists, steeped in the traditions of the arts hitherto comprising foreign policy, this or any proposal of an international Government may appear chimerical. For it involves a complete reversal of ideas and practices. The very term " international " is no more than a century old, and though since then it has enjoyed an ever-widening vogue, it has always been regarded with suspicion as an interloper in the circles of diplomacy. Its standpoint and its fundamental assumptions alike would, to a European Foreign Minister or Ambassador, seem to imply a betrayal of the separate interests of his country which are by right his sole consideration in dealing with other States. If this type of man, imbued with this spirit of the past, is entrusted by the nations of Europe with the settlement of the terms of peace and the determination of the future relations of the Powers, all hope of ending or abating militarism and its inevitable sequel disappears. It is to quite other forces of persuasion and negotiation that we must turn for any prospect of success for our policy of internationalism. Hitherto the peoples have been willing to leave the conduct of such momentous matters in the hands of their *de facto* rulers to do as they think best. Will they be content to do so now that the dire consequences of this misplaced confidence are so evident? Will they give a perfectly free hand for the making of peace to the statesmen whose most recent record is that they have made this war, and whose plans for the future will consist in preparations for another war? For we have shown that the sole alternative to internationalism is militarism. Will the peoples allow their " ministers " to choose this alternative? Not, I think, if they can be made to realize what that alternative means. And they will realize it by most convincing demonstrations.

Not only will there be around them the human and material wreckage of the war for reminders, but every people will be immediately confronted by the economic consequences of war—poverty, high prices, enhanced taxation, insecurity of employment, and industrial disturbances of every kind. Take the case of Great Britain, probably the country which will have suffered relatively least of the belligerents, in life and limb, in material losses, and even in financial damages. Unless a peaceful future can be secured along the lines of international government and public law, the people of this country will, whatever shape the peace may take, be immediately confronted by the almost certain prospects of conscription, with a Protective system which shall secure as far as possible a self-sufficing British Empire. The immense expenses of British militarism upon the continental scale added to our navalism, with the even greater costs and damages involved by the abandonment of our Free Trade policy, will fall upon the country when it is already burdened by the payment of the interest of war loans of colossal size, and is struggling to recover from the industrial, commercial, and financial dislocations of the war economy. Such a solution will be a thought-compeller of no ordinary power. Whatever Government is in office will be at its wits' end for the necessary revenue, the well-to-do classes of former days will be faced by demands for a continuation of the full war taxes in times of peace, while the endeavours to impose a tariff on foods and other necessaries upon the workers in a depressed and disorganized labour market will bring revolution nearer to our doors than it has been for three centuries. If this is the solution for England, it will be incomparably more dangerous for France, for Germany, and for the other belligerent countries, while the neutrals will be all confronted with the same financial and economic problems upon a reduced scale, with the same bottomless pit of the new competition in armaments yawning before them. The path to peace, disarmament, and internationalism will be the only escape from ruin and revolution for all peoples and all classes. This simple fact will be the education of the political parties and their leaders. The full force of the self-preserving instincts of every class will for the first time be enlisted on the side of peace. The period of exhaustion which follows the war will afford sufficient time for the necessary propaganda and discussion that must precede those conferences of the nations from which the international arrangements will emerge. Is it possible that the people of this or any other civilized State will permit their Government to send representatives to these conferences free to reject all proposals for securing future peace and for the establishment of an effective concert of nations? At a time when the thoughts and eyes of all the world are fastened upon the performance of this one necessary task will the obsolescent traditions and secret intrigues of a handful of rulers and diplomatists be allowed to wreck it? The pressure of the popular needs and the plain penalties for their denial will act as midwife to this new birth in history. The body of internationalism will be born of this travail of the peoples in this the ripeness of time. In countries with representative Constitutions the pressure will be urged along the regular provided channels ;

where no such avenues are open an impassioned public sentiment, shared everywhere by the great majority of all social classes, will bring the necessary compelling power to bear upon their rulers. There is nothing mysterious or mystical in this conception of the operation of the political forces which will bring international government. They will be in effect a continuation and a redirection of the patriotic passions evoked in a war which to each belligerent people has appeared to be a struggle for the preservation of its national existence. Each people has been told that the war "forced upon it" was "a war to end war," and they will insist on the fulfilment of the prophecy. This is the answer I would give to the timid cavillers at our project of international government. The immensity of the need will evoke the necessary will and the faith and courage to essay the large experiment.

After all, does it involve so great an act of faith?

All nations will be confronted with the same alternatives, military domination and the reign of war, or internationalism and the reign of law. Can there be any doubt which they will choose? What they are asked to do is to insist that the same methods already applied to the settlement of all issues between individuals, groups of individuals, and the smaller societies of cities or provinces shall be extended to the case of the larger social units called States. Is the proposal to make this extension so obviously chimerical?

The new forces, however, must be expected to work unequally. Some nations will be readier than others, and bolder in the steps they are prepared to take. It is for this reason that some internationalists look to a little group of advanced liberal nations to take the lead. If Great Britain, France, and the United States, perhaps with Italy, the Scandinavian countries, and Holland and Switzerland, formed the nucleus of the International League, the strength of its position would be such as gradually to bring other nations to seek membership. But though it would doubtless be easier to set on foot such a league of liberal States, the project would be attended by heavy risks and disadvantages. The most obvious of these risks would be that so limited an alliance, instead of bringing in the other nations one by one, might lead them to combine in another group, so restoring all the dangers of a Balance of Power. In any case, so long as such powerful States as Russia, Germany, Japan, were not included, the aggressive policy they would be capable of wielding, singly or in combination, would compel the Western Alliance to maintain so powerful a defensive force that the benefits of a League of Peace would be most inadequately realized. Moreover, most of the gravest problems of international politics would remain outside the area of pacific settlement. Closer regard to "real" politics makes it evident that, unless the great military Empires of Germany and Russia are members of the Confederation at the outset, the security for peace and for a reduction of armaments will be but slight. The case of Germany is, of course, the more critical, and that for two reasons. For the Russian Government, though based upon autocracy and with only the bare foundations of a popular Constitution, has shown both at The Hague and elsewhere strong leanings towards the realization of advanced internationalism. Whether as a recurring idealist streak in Tsardom or as a broader policy, this Russian liberality in international relations is not to be ignored. Moreover, though the recent association with France and Great Britain can easily be overrated as a pledge of future friendship, the war-alliance would certainly render it unlikely that Russia would remain outside a peace-alliance formed soon after the terms of the peace-settlement are reached. But the presence of Russia in an alliance in which the other two principal European members were her recent war-allies would give a sinister meaning to a professing peace-alliance if Germany remained outside. It would have the appearance of a continuance of the war-alliance against Germany and Austria, and the course of events would tend to convert that appearance into the substance of the arrangement, blasting all the higher hopes and aspirations, as was the case with the confederation of a century ago, formed to secure the peace of Europe after the Napoleonic war.

The admission of Germany to membership of the League is a prime condition of its success. No victory of the Allies in this war, however signal, can "crush" German militarism. Only by enlisting Germany as an equal member of the new international order will it be possible to achieve this object, either for Germany or for Europe at large. For Germany outside the League, though reduced to temporary impotence, would still retain its military spirit, and the Prussian military caste would be all the better enabled to hold their prestige and once again to muster the entire resources of the nation for the struggle against the ring of enemies around it. If, as is obviously true, the Germans alone can crush German militarism, they can only do so on condition that Germany becomes a member of the League. The objection that no confidence could be placed in Germany's fidelity to her pledges, however valid, cannot outweigh the danger of leaving her outside to plot and intrigue for the weakening of the League or the creation of a counter-League. Inside the League the German nation would have a stronger stimulus than any other to "crush" that Prussianism which had proved so much more disastrous to them than to their enemies. Those who feel so confident that Germany would refuse to enter such a League, however broken in immediate power, ignore the overwhelming evidences that even in Germany the people at large were goaded into militarism and war by their fears, and that the offensive motives which may have actuated their rulers and generals were not the dominant motives of the German people. It is important that these considerations shall be duly weighed in the formulation of the terms of peace. For it is incomparably better for the future of Europe to make such terms as are likely to incline the people of Germany to force their Government to enter the Confederation than to impose conditions which, by feeding a lasting passion of revenge, will strengthen the hold of Prussian militarism upon the Germans, and keep the great mid-European nation a permanent barrier to a peaceful future.

It is, indeed, obvious that, if public law is to be established on a basis of international government, not only the present belligerents but all the Great Powers if possible should be brought in. But here we enter at once a field of wide divergences of opinion and of sentiment. So far, we have treated internationalism as if it were a European problem. But among the belligerents is Japan, which will necessarily be represented at the Peace Conference from which the larger international proposals would naturally emanate, and which could hardly be excluded from the subsequent arrangements. Indeed, two non-European Powers must now be added to the six European which have hitherto conventionally figured as the Great Powers, viz. Japan and the United States. From discretion, if for no higher reason, it would seem important to secure, if possible, the inclusion of these non-European Powers. Indeed, all the deeper considerations of world-policy which we have already invoked confirm the view that an attempt to treat Europe as a separate political system would be mischievous. There are, of course, reasons which might conceivably deter both non-European Powers from desiring to enter such an international Government as we have indicated. For both the United States and Japan stand in a special relation of political and economic influence towards great neighbouring countries which are upon a lower level of strength and development. The ill-defined Monroe doctrine has made some recent extensions which are difficult to reconcile with the formal independence and integrity of South American States. Might not the Government and citizens of the United States have qualms lest their special claims and interests upon their continent might be disregarded by the instruments of an impartial international Government? This difficulty might seem graver still if the South American States themselves were admitted as equal members of the international society. But there are many grounds for thinking that the presence of the United States is as essential to the ultimate success of a League as that of Germany or of Great Britain. Some of these grounds are narrowly prudential. If the United States were not included, her political and economic interests would of necessity be concentrated more and more upon the American continent, and a new and injurious significance might come to attach to Canning's famous saying that he had called a new world into being in order to redress the balance of the old. If the United States were left to form a separate confederation of American States, although amiable relations might eventually be established between this and the European organization, an interim period of misunderstandings and suspicions might greatly impede the progress of disarmament and the security of peace. But there are broader considerations likely to weigh with the Government and people of the United States in favour of participation in an international alliance. Her internal development, as regards industry and population, has already removed her from the category of new countries content with the simple economy of bartering their surplus of foods and raw materials against the finished manufactured products of older countries. The economic status of the United States is less and less that of Canada and Argentina, more and more that of Great Britain, Holland, or Germany. Her merchants, manufacturers, and financiers must look henceforth to compete with Europeans in all parts of the world for the sale of their manufactured goods and for the investment of their capital. "The open door" and the world-politics involved in that phrase must count more every year in the calculations of American statesmen and business men. Indeed, it is already obvious that the intelligence of America has firmly grasped these truths of her new situation, and that she is preparing rapidly to recast her political ideas and valuations in accordance with the requirements of the new era. Her far-sighted business men perceive that the great economic future of the country depends upon ability to compete successfully and upon a large scale of enterprise in the general business of world-commerce and world-development. They will clearly recognize the advantage of entering a system of political internationalism designed to secure equality of economic opportunities for all nations and an impartial equitable settlement of all differences that may arise. For after a brief temptation to try the dangerous and costly path of protectionist Imperialism, the country has definitely rejected this policy. No large trend of American opinion favours the acquisition of colonies with subject races and the swollen militarism and navalism which such a policy evokes. The temper and traditions of the American people are pacific, and if they see a way of living upon terms of security and justice with other nations they will take it. The lesson of this European outbreak in its reactions upon their trade and politics will dispose them more strongly to this pacific course. For the peril of the alternative is already brought vividly before them, not only in trade damage and the risks which a neutral suffers of being drawn into the fray, but in the bold endeavours of the militarists in their midst to impose their naval and military projects on the nation. The only effective answer to this attempt is internationalism. For it is no more possible for the United States to hope to preserve a splendid isolation in the future than for Great Britain. Either, therefore, she must succumb to the demand for powerful defensive forces and a strong foreign policy or she must come into the International Society. Most of her leading statesmen, lawyers, and publicists have not hesitated to declare for justice, sanity, and internationalism. Nor have they waited for this war to avow their sentiments. The public opinion of educated America is already strongly organized for the acceptance of international ideals, and the part taken by American public men, both at The Hague and elsewhere, in urging the realization of these ideals has been one of higher faith and courage than that of any other nation. Finally, there is the consideration that the United States is in a position of peculiar influence and responsibility for the furtherance of this great end. The greatest of the neutral Powers in this war, it must fall to her, if not indeed to take the formal step of bringing the belligerents together for a discussion of peace terms, at any rate to exercise a strong and helpful influence in the subsequent policy of reconstruction. Indeed, the presence in the conferences of the one Great Power which enters without bloodstained hands and with feelings inflamed neither by triumph nor bitterness will be so evidently helpful that any endeavour to confine the settlement within the European system will rightly be regarded as a wrecking policy. America, alike in the make-up of her population, the liberality of her ideas, and the conscious declaration of her sympathies, possesses at present a larger measure of the international mind than any other nation, and since she is destined to play a growing part in the affairs of the world, her faith and courage should be great assets in the initial work of laying a true foundation of international institutions.

The first aim of the internationalists might be to obtain the adhesion to their main proposals of as many as possible among the eight Great Powers and the minor European States, leaving open the question of the immediate or the later accession of the other States which are recognized as entitled to representation at the Hague Conferences, or which may have a reasonable claim to be represented there. The number of nations entering the international experiment at the outset is not the prime condition of success. For if all, or nearly all, the great civilized nations can be brought in, the actual strength and the prestige of internationalism will exert an educative pressure of constantly increasing strength upon the peoples and Governments which remain outside. Apart from the preliminary sacrifice of false national pride involved in any measure of internationalism, the real crux consists in discovering some acceptable basis of the representation of nations in the International Council and its instruments of government. Where nations come together in a League or an Alliance, for the purposes of some closely defined common or mutual services, their action has been that of equal independent units. Though in the Conferences which such arrangements involve certain of the signatory Powers have usually arrogated to themselves a directing influence, resting in the last resort upon superior size and strength, the formal structure and proceedings of their Conferences do not commonly carry evidence of such discrimination.[1] Even where closer and more permanent relations were planned there would be a strong disposition, at any rate among the smaller Powers, to insist upon retaining this status of equality and its implication of independence. However large the powers accorded to the federal control in a federation of States, equality of representation might be regarded as a prescriptive right. To transgress this usage and to insist upon some other basis of representation, resting, not on independent sovereignty but upon some measure of the relative importance or competency of the co-operating Powers, would be likely to arouse suspicion and a fear lest what in

[1] In the Conferences of the "Grand Alliance" the tendency, however, of a little inner group, shifting in composition, to take over the initiative or direction and to form separate inner compacts was an important and a most disturbing one.

its first intent claimed to be a federation of States (a *Staaten-Bund*) should turn out to be the very different structure of a federal State (a *Bundes-Staat*). Yet this suspicion and this fear must be firmly faced if our scheme of internationalism, upon any scale of efficiency, is to be realized. For whatever theoretical validity may be claimed for the view that all States, irrespective of size or territory, strength, population, or civilized status, ought to be equally represented upon the Council of Nations and its Courts and Committees, no such international arrangements as we contemplate could be operated upon such a basis. Nor is it reasonable that they should. For this doctrine of absolute equality evidently rests upon an over-stressing of that very factor of absolute State independence which it is the purpose of our policy to moderate and to overrule. Though the initial coming together for the establishment of our international arrangements is an act of separate sovereignty, a voluntary contract between equals, a certain cession of that very equality for future purposes of co-operation is indispensable to the realization of these purposes. Now, in the case of a number of nations entering an enduring compact to undertake in common the important deliberative, judicial, and executive functions ascribed to them in the schemes we have discussed, absolute equality of representation would be an unsound and unreasonable basis. That Denmark or Servia, not to mention Monaco and San Marino, should have precisely the same number of voices in the Council as Great Britain, Russia, or the United States could hardly be advocated, even by the stoutest champions of small nationalities. It may perhaps be said that international justice and wisdom is as important for a small as for a great people, and that if small nations are liable to be outvoted by big nations with more representatives, the tyranny of arms which they have often suffered in the past will only be replaced by a constitutional tyranny equally objectionable. But there is no substance in this plea. In the first place, it is not true that equal representation tends to secure for any little nation juster or wiser international treatment. Quite the contrary. Equal representation will continually keep alive and emphasize the national as distinguished from the international point of view, and tend to introduce a group-nationalism into the deliberations and the policy of the Council. The big nations, with their own axes to grind, would be continually angling and intriguing for the support of a sufficient number of small States to carry through their particular projects, as was the case with Prussia and Austria in the German Confederation as established by the Congress of Vienna. Genuinely international policy requires that the interests, capacities, and needs, not of sovereign States, but of peoples, shall prevail. Now, it is idle to pretend that number of population is not a relevant consideration where the interests of peoples are at stake, or that the welfare of Montenegro is as important, in the human sense, as that of Russia. Even if our international policy were destined to have no more unity of purpose than was attainable by the respective pulls of its constituent national units, it would be better that the representation of these units should be weighted by some populational allowance. For, putting the matter at its worst, it would be better for the interests of the great nations to prevail than for those of the small nations, not because a great nation is more likely to be in the right, but because it is better for a larger number of human beings to have their way than for a smaller. But the case for population representation is, of course, far stronger, if we are entitled to assume some genuine sense of justice and some real regard for the good of the society of nations in the deliberations and the policy of our International Council. For if, as I should insist, the success of this arrangement depends upon getting together in the Council the ablest, most experienced, and most public-spirited men which the nations can furnish, it would be the extremity of folly to take precisely the same number from each nation. It may, indeed, well be the case that some smaller nation, such as Holland or Switzerland by reason of its high standard of education or other advantages of position, contains a much larger quota of men fitted for such international service than some countries with a far larger population. That may be a valid ground for qualifying any populational basis by some other tests of fitness. But it is not a reason for ignoring population as a determinant factor in the problem. Other things equal (i.e. education, industrial status, geographical position, etc.), a country with a larger population will be in a position to make a larger contribution of suitable men to our International Council than a country with a smaller population. Indeed, the qualitative economy of personnel is so obvious that I should not have laboured it thus far were it not desirable to show that in this instance reason and justice are on the side of the great battalions. For this purpose I retain to the last what the practical man will regard as an all-sufficient argument, viz. the evident impossibility of getting the Great Powers into any sort of international arrangement in which their "greatness" was not recognized. Though pride and selfishness may enter into this claim for larger representation, that claim is not intrinsically unjust or unreasonable. The aggregate of welfare contained in the great nations is a greater human value than that contained in the small nations, and its capacity for international service is also greater.

Though it is possible that small nations, partly from pride of nationality, partly from genuine fears, may at first look askance at proposals for a Council in which a handful of Great Powers may appear to be supreme, and may even decline to enter into what they may consider as a spider's web, I think that reflection will wear down this early attitude of suspicion and show them that there is more safety inside than outside this society of nations. For if there were a general disposition on the part of Great Powers to "domineer" in the International Council and to override the equal rights of small nations, would not the latter be in a far stronger position if they organized a constitutional resistance as members of the League or Federation than if they permitted the justice of their case to go by default and trusted to an armed defence foredoomed to failure. But the supposition of such a general policy of oppression on the part of Great Powers, operative so as to unite them against a small nation or a group of small nations, in any given issue, is itself unwarranted. On the contrary, history shows that the mere "sympathy" of greatness does not keep Great Powers in accord, or lead them to support the encroachments of one among their number. Fear, jealousy, and suspicion have ever been more rife among great than among little Powers, and the notion that the party politics of internationalism would run on mere lines of size has no ground in the realities of the modern situation. A Holland, Switzerland, or Poland would be far securer of its rights if it had representatives within the Council and a right of appeal to the International Court than if it hugged a self-centred and necessarily precarious policy of isolation. Such considerations would, I think, certainly prevail to bring in the smaller European nations.

Having once accepted the general principle of a representation roughly proportionate to the size and population of the constituent nations, no present purpose is served by endeavouring to work out any close basis for such representation.[1] At the outset of the experiment such a question would evidently be one for compromise and special arrangement rather than for a rigorous logic of proportion. A good deal would depend upon the contemplated size of the International Council, and

[1] The representation adopted for the International Prize Court at The Hague, though hardly acceptable as it stands, would form a serviceable starting-point for such an inquiry.

this in its turn would hinge partly upon the number of the constituent nations, partly upon the scope of the international Government. If the more modest, but to my mind less effective, experiment of a simple League of Peace were adopted, a small, compact Council of nominees of the respective Governments would probably be formed. For any special labours of inquiry such a Council might co-opt the services of experts, so keeping the dimensions of the international body such as to facilitate close personal intercourse and understanding. In such a case it would probably suffice if each of the Great Powers appointed, say, three representatives and the smaller Powers one or two.

If, however, the international experiment were made upon the wider basis, provision should be made for a more generous representation, so that each nation might have upon the International Council some fairly adequate reflection of its various capabilities and interests. Although it would be impossible for such a body, in effect an International Parliament, to prescribe the method of election or appointment to be adopted by the several nations, those committed in their national affairs to the principle of popular election would probably desire to find some method by which this democratic principle might be extended to the wider area of government. If direct popular election of the national representatives for the International Council were deemed impracticable or inconvenient, some mode of selection through an electoral college, partly elected by localities, partly by professions, trades, and labour unions, might be substituted. In the more liberal

Western nations, at any rate, it would seem most desirable that the type of man chosen for a representative should be drawn, not from the diplomatic or distinctively official class, but from those who have risen to public influence and eminence by practical sagacity and experience in the handling of affairs. The able parliamentarian rather than the expert administrator is the fit representative of a people that desires to have the breath of popular self-government play through the new international institutions. For the chief peril confronting such an experiment at the outset will be the endeavour of the diplomatic caste of each nation to capture the national representation, and to introduce the poison of the old statecraft into the new international system. This peril can best be met by the resolute determination of the democratic peoples to appoint as their representatives men untainted by the theories and the practices which have fostered ill-will and dissensions among nations in the past. The presence of such men upon the Council, imbued with the true spirit of internationalism, will be required to counteract the machinations of the representatives of less enlightened Powers, who may be disposed in the initial stage of the experiment to assume the position of a "State's right" party, suspicious and perhaps obstructive of the wider functions, upon the successful performance of which the progress of internationalism depends.

The considerations here adduced have a bearing upon a practical issue of great importance, viz. the part to be taken by the existing structure of the Hague Tribunals and Conventions in our larger schemes of international government. Would it not be best to build upon the actual foundations of arbitral and judicial procedure and the deliberative and quasi-legislative bodies represented by the Hague Congresses, Conventions, and Courts? If more continuity, larger powers, and stronger sanctions could be secured for this international instrument, it would appear a truly sound economy to use it for the larger work of international government. It is but the shallowest and most ignorant criticism which regards the present war and the breakdown of international laws and conventions it has exhibited as a testimony to the failure and futility of Hague pacifism. For no body of men recognized so clearly the insufficiency of existing rules and sanctions of international law to secure peace as those who have been closely associated with the conferences and constructive proposals of The Hague. Though the external and the psychological conditions will be greatly changed when Europe is once again upon a peace basis, it would be a grave error to ignore the important contribution which the experience of The Hague can make towards the solution of the problems of international relations that will burst with novel force upon the mind of the politicians and citizens of every civilized country. At The Hague there exists something more than the rudiments of an international judicial and legislative system, and on the face of things it would seem more reasonable to develop this system and to endow it with the larger executive powers that will be needed than either to erect a brand-new edifice, or merely to utilize the Hague Courts for the arbitral and judicial work delegated to them by a Council which, neither in its constitution nor in its place of meeting, preserves a continuity with the earlier experiment in internationalism.

There are, however, as our discussion has already indicated, grave difficulties to be encountered in moulding the existing constitution of the Hague Congresses and Courts into the form which seems essential to the success of our larger scheme. The forty-four States represented at The Hague meet on a basis of absolute equality and complete independence: no decision of a majority, however large, is binding on a minority, however small, and there is no cession to the international assembly of any power by the several States. To convert this voluntary gathering of equal Powers, each retaining its unfettered liberty in dealing with every practical proposal for co-operative action, into the International Council we have sketched, might prove impracticable. Indeed, a complete conversion, in the sense of an incorporation of the forty-four States in our new plan of international government, would be virtually impossible. For it might be taken as axiomatic that the Great Powers would not enter the close organic union here proposed if their influence and will were liable to be overborne by the numerical strength and voting power of a large number of relatively small and backward States, including those of Asia and South America. On the other hand, *amour propre* and possibly a sense of danger would certainly deter some of the smaller States from accepting a deposition from their existing equal status at The Hague. If, therefore, the Hague Congress were taken as a starting-point, a satisfactory Council could only be formed by the voluntary agreement of a number of States transforming themselves into an inner league, with a separate proportional representation and a constitution of their own. The continuity of a Council thus formed with the machinery of The Hague would be very slight, and its ability or willingness to utilize or expand even the existing Courts (upon which nations not included in this league would have representatives) would be very doubtful. It is thus evident that a great and difficult transformation would be necessary to accommodate the machinery of The Hague to the larger work of international government. If, however, these difficulties can be surmounted, it would be highly desirable to secure the formal and the real advantages which continuity with these early experiments in internationalism would afford.

In conclusion, one important counsel of discretion deserves mention. In order to abate as much as possible the suspicions or fears which may be entertained by certain States whose early presence on the Council is urgently desirable, the right of withdrawal or secession after reasonable notice should be specifically recognized in the terms of any treaty or convention by which the international arrangements are brought into being. Nations should be entirely free to withdraw, provided that the terms of notice are such as to preclude any nation from withdrawing in order to avoid the fulfilment of her treaty obligations in respect of any particular matter regarding which her conduct might be in question.

CHAPTER XI

THE INTERNATIONAL MIND

STARTING from the assumption that it was urgently desirable for nations to try to establish such relations with one another as may avert the likelihood of war, secure a sensible relief in the burden of armaments, and provide some better way of settling differences and enabling nations to co-operate for common purposes, I have set forth a series of proposals in an order of increasing dimensions and complexity. None of these proposals strictly belongs to the terms of peace which will conclude this war, though the meeting of Powers to settle and to sign the Peace Treaty may take the initial steps towards the establishment of some more permanent arrangements for securing future peace.

But since the feasibility of all the proposals we discuss involves, as we have seen, the voluntary co-operation of leading members of the European groups which have just issued from a deadly conflict, the terms and spirit of the settlement are of vital importance. The vanquished party must, of course, suffer heavily in terms of blood and money, in the restitution of ravished territory, and in the temporary loss of military and naval strength. Such are the normal fortunes of an unsuccessful war. A nation thus beaten does not naturally harbour lasting resentment against the conquerors, or cherish projects of revenge. Some measure of humiliation is necessarily inflicted upon its military and its ruling classes actively responsible for the terrible sufferings of their people, but the spirit of the people suffers no such embitterment. Very different, however, would be the result of a policy of dismemberment, or of any attempt permanently to cripple the economic or even the military recovery of the nation. History teaches no clearer lesson than the folly and futility of such a vindictive policy. But I am here only concerned with its most deplorable result. The dismemberment or national degradation of Germany would blast all hopes of a pacific future for the world by planting a permanent danger zone in the centre of Europe, which would keep that quarter of the globe an armed camp and a perpetual area of intrigue. Complete victory might enable the Allies for a time to impose rigorous limits upon German militarism. But history shows the ultimate futility and mischief of such a policy. It fosters rancour and revenge in the subject nation, obliges the dominant nations to maintain strong forces and incessant vigilance, and ensures an outbreak on a favourable opportunity. Herein lies the all-importance of a settlement based, not upon short-range military expediency but upon a far-sighted and comprehensive statesmanship, having due regard to the reactions of the settlement upon the larger constructive policy of internationalism.

But given these preliminary conditions for our

experiments towards international government, how far is it feasible and desirable to seek to go? The questions of feasibility and desirability are not identical. Many who would desire to take the most advanced of our proposals, could they persuade themselves of its feasibility, are deterred even from discussing it, for fear that such discussion may discredit their advocacy of some smaller proposal which they consider to be really practicable. But I submit that at the present stage of consideration we should be wise to claim a larger liberty than may be possible later on when the issue becomes one of immediate politics.

The various proposals we have examined are not clearly distinct from one another. They sometimes overlap and sometimes receive special enlargements in the hands of particular advocates. But in general they fall under three categories. First come those based upon the narrow "practical" suggestion that States shall band together to give mutual guarantees against all wars. Provisions for settling disputes by arbitral or other means are sometimes added. But they remain subsidiary to the "stop-war" motive. Next come the proposals primarily concerned with methods and instruments of conciliation and of arbitration, based primarily upon appeals to reason, the sense of justice, and public opinion. Some of these proposals contain material guarantees for the performance of certain undertakings, but they do not rest upon a binding prohibition of all war. The third class of proposals aims at an agreement of Powers to establish an international government by means of a permanent representative International Council exercising powers of arbitration and conciliation, with executive authority to enforce arbitral or judicial awards and decisions of the Council, and to repress attacks made by any of the treaty-Powers upon any other treaty-Power, or by any outside Power upon any of the treaty-Powers. Though the first object of this international Government would be the security of peace and the maintenance of existing public law, the evolution of events in international relations would require that certain prescribed legislative powers should be conferred upon the Government for the improved co-operation of nations in all activities in which their common interests are involved. If the public law of nations is ever to be set upon the same secure basis as the municipal law of every civilized State, some such formal international Legislature as is here contemplated must be brought into being.

Now, my argument has evidently been addressed to persuade readers to direct their hopes and efforts to the attainment of the most advanced of these positions, chiefly because the less advanced positions, though perhaps more easily attainable, do not contain effective guarantees of peace or furnish sufficient motives to secure an early or a lasting reduction of armaments. Indeed, in view of the evident ineffectiveness of these positions, I even doubt whether they can rightly be considered more attainable. For when the political mind of the nation is fairly at grips with the situation I am disposed to think that it will brush aside all more timid and tentative devices as flimsy barriers against a sudden onrush of the war spirit, and, taking for its indispensable test the effectiveness of guarantees, will make for the bolder policy of international government.

But it is well to face the immense difficulties which beset the path of those who work towards the attainment even of the least advanced position. The present intellectual atmosphere is one of profound scepticism. All the forces of reason, justice, goodwill, and common interest, upon which most men had relied as efficient brakes upon the war-chariot, have ignominiously failed. The complex informal web of international relations through commerce and finance has proved as feeble a defence of peace as the more formal bonds of treaty and of international law. How, in the face of this collapse of all pacific forces and arrangements, can we honestly expect to attain security by any international agreement or any system of "paper" guarantees? Each nation in the future, more evidently even than in the past, must trust to its own strong right hand and to such comrades in arms as are bound to it by common fears and common enmities!

This very natural scepticism of all peace arrangements on the part of "the practical man" is the immediate barrier. Its "nothing-can-be-done" attitude serves to paralyse thought. Nor is it possible by mere argument to break through this incredulity. One can only trust that when the "practical man" realizes the full material and moral costs of his counsel of despair he will bestir himself to find some way of avoiding payment. He will then discover the necessity of moving along some such paths of business arrangements as we have sketched, and will insist upon applying with rigour the test of effective guarantees.

But the naïve scepticism of the man in the street is fortified among the educated classes by two types of objection to all large schemes of international arrangements which demand fuller consideration.

The first consists in the conscious or unconscious acceptance of a half-legal, half-philosophical theory of the National State as the final stage in the process of social evolution. The juridical conception of absolute independence and sovereignty for the State is supported on the side of social philosophy by the doctrine that "consciousness of kind," and the community of experience necessary for effective realization of common purposes, are confined within the limits of the nation.[1] Thus no reliable basis for effective inter-State or international co-operation is furnished by the actual experience of life. The national State, being thus the largest type of social grouping, cannot rightly enter into any permanently valid engagements, with other States that impair its complete sovereignty. The State in effect is a moral absolute. Applied with logical rigour, this conception of the State carries with it that domination over individual lives, and that dispensation from all external duties or obligations, which we are discovering to be the inspiring genius of the German "Real-Politik." In this discovery we are mistaken. Germany, indeed, among modern States has carried farthest in theory and in practice the doctrine of the supre-

[1] See Bosanquet's "Theory of the State," and Giddings' "The Principles of Sociology."

macy of the State over the person of its citizens. But, as regards the relation of the State to other States, though German historians, philosophers, and statesmen have formulated the absolutist doctrine with more rigour, they have not invented it. Its practical implication that any action may be justified by "necessity" or "reason of state" was formulated by Macchiavelli, by Hobbes, and by a whole series of British, French, and Italian political thinkers. Everything we are condemning in Treitschke as a specifically German vice of thought is old as the hills alike for theory and for practice. A single illustration may serve to make this clear. Nothing more shocked "the conscience of the civilized world" in the conduct of this war than the German contention that the "necessity" of her situation warranted her brutal assault upon the neutrality of Belgium. Yet our sudden, unprovoked attack upon Copenhagen in 1806 without declaring war was justified by our Government of that day in language almost identical with that employed last year by the German Chancellor. It ran as follows:—

> Royal Proclamation. While he [the King] laments the cruel necessity which has obliged him to have recourse to acts of hostility against a nation with which it was His Majesty's most earnest desire to have established the relations of common interest and alliance, His Majesty feels confident that in the eyes of Europe and the world the justification of his conduct will be found in the commanding and indispensable duty, paramount to all others among the obligations of a sovereign, of providing while there was yet time, for the immediate security of his people.

In a word, *Salus reipublicæ suprema lex*, a doctrine which is the negation of all law.

It is this false, immoral doctrine, inimical to humanity, that a State is an absolute morally self-contained being, living in the world with other similar beings, but owing no duties to them and bound by no obligations that it may not break on the plea of necessity, which is the fundamental vice embedded in that foreign policy the fruits of which we are now reaping. If nations were in point of fact self-contained, materially and morally, living in splendid or even in brutish isolation, this doctrine of States or Governments might be tenable. But they are not. On the contrary, their intercourse and interdependence for every kind of purpose, economic, social, scientific, recreative, spiritual, grows continually closer. Hence the doctrine of State sovereignty and independence grows continually falser. The facts of modern life force nations to come into close and frequent relations. But statecraft provides no intellectual or moral basis for these relations. International law and usage are indeed experiments towards such a basis, but, possessing neither authoritative origin nor effective guarantee, they are liable at any time to be thrown aside by the dominance of "State necessity." But the inhumanity of foreign policy is not confined to this obsolete conception of the moral sovereignty and independence of the State. It is expressed with equal significance in the mode of envisaging the State which prevails in foreign policy and in diplomatic intercourse. States are represented in their capacity of "Powers." This reduces the absolutism of the State to terms of military force. It is the literal rendering of that doctrine of "the will to power" which we affect to believe that the teaching of Nietzsche has imposed on Germany. So long as diplomatic intercourse is conducted between "Powers" it is difficult to get on to any plane of human friendliness or common purpose. How can it be expected that Foreign Ministers and Ambassadors, drawn almost exclusively by close selection from the fighting, ruling caste of their respective nations, and inured to traditions of military prowess and personal dominion, should be able or willing to release themselves from the clutches of the "Power" concept which is enshrined in every official act they perform or document they sign?

The significance of words, especially in the art of diplomacy, is indeed proverbial. When nations enter a formal agreement with one another, they are "the Signatory Powers." When they deign, for the nonce, to quit their splendid isolation, they form "a Concert of the Powers." Some of them at any given epoch are "Great Powers"—and their greatness is the measure of the fighting forces they can command. But the most sinister employment of the term is contained in the phrase which, ever since it was invented by the most unscrupulous of English statesmen,[1] has been the supreme engine of international mischief, the Balance of Power. So long as nations are conceived as Powers, and foreign policy as the manipulation of Power by statesmen to whom the exercise and increase of the power of the nation is the supreme criterion of success, no stable international arrangements are possible. For though the term Balance

[1] Sir Robert Walpole.

of Power suggests a stable equilibrium, it only does so by a complete falsification of the situation. In a purely statical world such a mechanical balance might be attainable. In the changing world we know such a balance can only endure for a passing moment. But it is not necessary to labour the folly of pretending to solve the greatest of human problems in terms of statical mechanics. For history shows that this expression Balance of Power is nothing else than the core of diplomatic falsehood. The statesmen who employ it do not want to preserve a just balance, but always to tip the scale in favour of the Power or group of Powers they represent.

To diplomatists the relations between nations are thus grounded in assumptions of antagonism of interests, deeply embedded in the art and language they employ. Alike the theory, the practice, and the personnel of diplomacy and foreign policy are vitiated by this falsehood and inhumanity.

But associated with it is another vice which helps to poison foreign policy. It consists in the control of that policy by special business groups and interests within each nation for purposes of private gains. Tariffs and other protective measures, directed to benefit a section of a nation and to damage a section of another nation ; preferential or exclusive trade with colonies and protectorates, the struggle for treaty ports, mining and railway concessions in backward countries, for banks and loans to foreign Governments, and in general for all lucrative propositions of "development," have in recent times more and more occupied the energies of Foreign Offices and of diplomatists, and have continually inflamed jealousies, suspicions, and antagonisms among the Governments of the competing interests. Some of this business direction of foreign policy is definitely bad. The whole protective policy is, of course, doubly injurious to the nation that employs it, for, while it diminishes the total real income of the nation, it damages its political relations with other nations. But still more disastrous to pacific relations has been the policy of intrigue and diplomatic pressure pursued on behalf of groups of concession-mongers and financiers by the Foreign Offices of commercial and investing nations. For though some of this business may be beneficial to the general trade and industry of the nation, there is not the slightest guarantee that this will be the case. The pressure exercised by financial groups through their respective Governments on foreign States or Protectorates to effect profitable loans, to obtain land, railway, or mining concessions, or to secure spheres of business enterprise, is the key to the understanding of the dealings of European States in recent years in Egypt, South Africa, China, Persia, Morocco, and most other undeveloped countries. In some instances the net results of the political and economic intervention thus brought about may have been advantageous to the intervening nation and to the nation subject to this intervention, in other cases not. But the point is that the foreign policy has in every case been motived and directed, not by any national interest at all but by the particular interests of small groups of financiers, investors, and merchants out for private gain, and seeking to use the diplomatic and armed resources of their country to further their business purposes. Their prostitution of the State to private interests, with the international jealousies and hostilities involved, is directly traceable to the secret autocratic methods of the Foreign Offices, and of the close personal sympathy which exists between the political conception of the State, as an instrument of power, and the commercial conception of it as an instrument for pushing private profitable enterprises.

The two complementary parts of this vicious theory and practice find their most appropriate union in the place occupied in foreign policy by the armament trade. Here the entire political philosophy of power is reduced to an impudent simplicity. We have seen that, for purposes of foreign policy, a State regards itself as a Power. But it is not the self-sufficing being that it represents itself to be. It is not a Power in itself: it buys its power in expensive bits from private business firms, whose interest it is to stimulate it continually to buy more power in the shape of ships, guns, ammunition, etc., and to pay whatever prices each of these firms, in agreement with its few sham competitors, arranges to demand from its Government. Here we have powerful, highly organized industries directly interested in feeding the fears, suspicions, and enmities of nations, and enabled by the powerful personal influence of their carefully chosen directors and their shareholders to bring pressure upon their Governments to put larger and larger quantities of public money into their private pockets.

The crowning feature of this audacious conspiracy against the peace of Europe is found in the "internationalism" of the armament trade. The great armament firms of one nation are so linked up by interlocking directorates, trade agreements, common ownership of secret processes, and by their common interest in fanning and feeding international animosities, as to present an economic phenomenon unique in history, an international trade which lives and thrives by manufacturing hate and the instruments of hate between nations. For these vendors of power are as cosmopolitan in their markets as in their directorates. Germans and Austrians have been sitting side by side with Britons, French, and Italians in the control of businesses which have been supplying our present enemies as well as our Allies with the implements of war. Inside each nation these little business groups of war-traders have been incessantly at work, advising and stimulating the military and naval departments by true or false reports of the preparations which other nations (also by their advice and aid) were making against them. Enjoying access to the military and naval secrets of each country, they were in an excellent position to supply both goods and information to other War Offices and Admiralties, and so keep business humming. That the "Great Powers" should have allowed these private profiteering cosmopolitan monsters thus to prey upon their very vitals is the culminating modern instance of capitalist control of politics.[1]

[1] See Mr. H. N. Brailsford's "The War of Steel and Gold" Chap. IX, and for a more detailed exposition, Mr. G. H. Perris's, "The War Traders" and pamphlets by Mr. Walton Newbold.

We now see what the theory and the practice of foreign policy signify. The foreign relations which concern these ministers and diplomats are relations between Powers, which are in theory directed to secure balances by means of groupings based upon the supposed strength of military and naval force. This inhuman theory is disturbed and distorted in practice by the pulls and drives of business and caste interests and sentiments, commercial and financial power, armament firms, and the constant pressure of the "services" and would-be Empire-builders towards a spirited foreign and colonial policy. Such are the ineradicable vices of a foreign policy of Power, administered by a virtually self-appointed and uncontrolled bureaucracy.

Now it may be at once admitted that no internationalism of the order here contemplated can be achieved if this policy and this personnel remain intact. Unless foreign policy can be made to express the relation between Peoples, not between Powers, nothing is achieved. No attempt to work a Concert of Europe, a League of Peace, an International Council, by entrusting the constructive policy to members of the diplomatic castes of the several nations can prove other than disastrous.

This is the real lesson to be learned from the example of a century ago, which is pressed upon us by academic historians as proof of the Utopianism of all efforts after international government. Those who to-day are planning Leagues of Peace and other schemes of international confederation are confronted with a series of former projects and experiments directed to the same general ends, employing the same means and formulated in almost the same terms as those of to-day, and destined to complete and ignominious failure. When the Treaty of Utrecht concluded the continental wars of the early eighteenth century, the moral and material havoc in Europe set men thinking upon the possibility of getting nations on to a stable footing of pacific relations. The ripest fruit of this thinking was the *Projet de Traité pour rendre la Paix Perpetuelle* of the Abbé de St. Pierre, published in 1713. A League of Peace for the maintenance of public law was to be formed with the following provisions :

1. The Sovereigns are to contract a perpetual and irrevocable alliance, and to name plenipotentiaries to hold, in a determined spirit, a permanent diet or congress, in which all differences between the contracting parties are to be settled by arbitration or judicial decision.

2. The number of the Sovereigns sending plenipotentiaries to the congress is to be specified, together with those who are to be invited to accede to the treaty. The presidency of the congress is to be exercised by the Sovereigns in turn at stated intervals, the order of rotation and term of office being carefully defined. In like manner the quota to be contributed by each to the common fund, and its method of collection, are to be carefully defined.

3. The Confederation thus formed is to guarantee to each of its members the sovereignty of the territories it actually possesses, as well as the succession, whether hereditary or elective, according to the fundamental laws of each country. To avoid disputes, actual possession and the latest treaties are to be taken as the basis of the mutual rights of the contracting Powers, while all future disputes are to be settled by arbitration of the Diet.

4. The Congress is to define the cases which would involve offending States being put under the ban of Europe.

5. The Powers are to agree to arm and take the offensive in common and at the common expense, against any State thus banned, until it shall have submitted to the common will.

6. The plenipotentiaries in congress, on instructions from their Sovereigns, shall have power to make such rules as they shall judge important with a view to securing for the European Republic and each of its members all possible advantages.

Though this proposal found no acceptance among the statesmen of the age, and was rejected as chimerical even by so free a thinker as Rousseau, it was destined to reappear under what seemed far more favourable circumstances a century later, when the fall of Napoleon broke once more the spell of militarism upon the Continent and stirred fresh hopes of the possibilities of a pacific future. Mr. Allison Phillips, in his valuable book, "The Confederation of Europe,"[1] shows how the allied Powers of Europe in their larger or smaller groupings endeavoured to incorporate the various provisions of St. Pierre in some practical scheme of co-operative union to keep the peace, and to guarantee public order in Europe.

The active will in these political experiments was that of the Tsar Alexander I, who from 1804 onwards kept this general idea of a European Confederation in the forefront of his political schemes. Though historical analogies can never safely be pressed far, there is much in the European situation of a century ago to remind us of the situation which will presently emerge when the military power of Germany is broken. Substituting Germany for France, the following response of Pitt in 1805 to Alexander's proposal of a

[1] Longmans, 1914.

European alliance is sufficiently suggestive of the general lines of settlement which are forming themselves to-day in many minds. After discussing the general desirability of a Concert, Pitt recites its objects, dividing them into the following three groups :

1. To release from the domination of France the territories conquered since the Revolution.

2. To form out of the countries thus released, with due regard to their peace and happiness, a barrier against future French aggression.

3. To establish, after the restoration of peace, a convention and guarantee for the mutual protection and security of the different Powers, and to establish in Europe a general system of public law.[1]

Pitt's remarks upon the most fundamental of these proposals, the third, deserve citation :—

"In order to make this security as perfect as possible, it seems necessary that at the time of the general pacification a treaty should be concluded, in which all the principal European Powers should take part, by which their possessions and their respective rights, as there established, should be fixed and recognized ; and these Powers should all engage reciprocally to protect and support each other against all attempts to violate it. This treaty would give to Europe a general system of public law and would aim at repressing, as far as possible, future attempts to trouble the general tranquillity, and, above all, to defeat every project of aggrandizement and ambition, such as those which have produced all the disasters by which Europe has

[1] Phillips, p. 36.

been afflicted since the unhappy era of the French Revolution." [1]

These views, first embodied in a Treaty of 1805 between Russia and Great Britain, became operative motives in European policy ten years later, and, with various restrictions and extensions as regards purposes and signatory nations, found expression in the entanglement of treaties and alliances which spread from 1814 through the succeeding decade, ending in the break-up of the Holy Alliance by the policy of Canning and the collapse of the tortuous endeavours to realize a Confederation of Europe.

This failure of effective and peaceable co-operation between European nations Mr. Phillips considers to be as inevitable to-day as it was a hundred years ago. The assumption that the changed conditions of to-day render possible a project for which Europe was not then ripe he dismisses as unwarranted.

He appears to hold that a general alliance of nations to impose and in the last resort enforce the public law of Europe, which all may have formally adopted, would be as impracticable as ever. For while it is possible that an *ad hoc* coalition of Great Powers might be able and prepared " to enforce the principles which now stand unanimously acknowledged by the Second Peace Conference of The Hague," it would be impossible to extend this coalition into " a universal union," based on " the general right of the world-organization to coerce its refractory members." For what, he asks, would then become of " the

[1] Phillips, p. 38.

sovereign independence of nations"? "Especially it would be the small States whose independence would be prejudiced; for though international law recognizes in them the equality of all sovereign States, no international system which should attempt to translate this theory into practice would survive. If, on the other hand, the voting power of the central 'directory' were to be proportioned to the size and importance of its constituent States, the result would be precisely such a hegemony of the Great Powers as was exercised by the Holy Alliance after 1815." The new Alliance, like the old, would be driven to interfere with "internal affairs." As Sir F. Pollock insists, "the effective working of an international federal system demands a far greater uniformity of political institutions and ideas among the nations of the world than at present exists."

Now, this is a really formidable indictment, the full force of which is contained in its final count. For it comes to this that, although modern civilization may have brought certain more liberal nations up to a level of justice and humanity which would express itself in the fair and equal treatment of Western nations in a Union, the consciousness of "power" would continue to impel certain other great nations to violate their treaty obligations, to exercise their will by voting power or force to the detriment of smaller nations, and to break through any limitations set upon the right of the Union to interfere in internal politics. In a word, it has been impossible to secure an equitable spirit of internationalism in a large heterogeneous alliance such as is proposed, in the past, and it must continue to be impossible in the future.

History, it is contended, thus supports political theory in insisting that the national State is a final product of social evolution, and that the political instinct of men has exhausted itself in attaining this goal. But before turning to the test of history, one is entitled to question the theoretical assumption. What is the worth of this assumption that the associative instincts and interests of men, which have gradually built up the fabric of the national State from smaller social units by fusion and co-operation, are precluded from carrying the process any farther by some absolute barriers of sovereignty and independence? Were not the smaller social units, which have in the past grown together into the present national States, once themselves little States, often as sovereign and as independent as the great States of to-day? If once separate tribes, cantons, and provinces, widely divergent from one another in economic structure, in civilized development, in language, and in political government, have been able to coalesce or to co-operate in a larger political union, why should not nations be able to do the same? It may, indeed, well be admitted that wide differences of political institutions render federation difficult. But they do not render it impossible.

Moreover, the changes of the last century, which to Mr. Phillips seem almost negligible, are in reality exceedingly important contributions towards the feasibility of such a federation. Not only have the rights of nationality and of local autonomy made great advances towards realization in the map of Europe, but the ideas and the sentiments which they embody are the common accepted doctrines of liberal thinkers in all countries, and their definite acknowledgment in the settlement of this war would be a powerful incentive towards that standardization of government which is so great a desideratum for the co-operation of free States. Every extension of effective self-government makes for the further assimilation of internal polities among the different nations. The institutions, central and local, in which such self-government expresses itself, exhibit among the free peoples of most countries striking resemblances, which are the natural products of community of human wants and efforts seeking expression in forms of self-government which in modern times become more and more consciously imitative. Nations and even their Governments are far nearer to one another in actual structure and in conscious tendencies than was the case a century ago, while their intercommunication of ideas and influences is immensely greater. Do these facts not count in considering the feasibility of carrying one stage farther the process of social evolution and in planning a Society of Nations?

But granting that nations are somewhat nearer to one another in their political arts and institutions than they were when Alexander projected his Grand Alliance, have they reached a degree of uniformity that will enable them to co-operate successfully in maintaining peace and public law? I agree that it is impossible to give with any confidence an affirmative reply, although the whole issue of the maintenance and progress of our civilization is here at stake. But equally I deny the right of historians and political philosophers to affirm the contrary. A State, or national society, may and often does contain within itself communities or localities widely discrepant in their culture, status, outlook, and local government. But though this diversity may sometimes weaken the State, it does not destroy it, and is quite consistent with an effective spirit of nationality permeating the whole structure and maintaining the requisite unity of national will. Indeed, so far as their political diversity is rooted in differences of local needs and conditions, it may be a source of strength, not of weakness. Why should not the same hold good of a society of nations, provided it is inspired by a sufficiently vigorous spirit of internationalism? We have already seen that the most powerful, varied, and distinctive growth of recent times has been that web of international relations, economic, social, scientific, philanthropic, which everywhere testifies to a liberal-mindedness and a community of interests and purposes transcending the limits of country and nation. These relations, though as yet thinly represented in the sphere of politics, have been educating an international mind. The elaborate and secure arrangements by which men, goods, letters, money, news are carried by a single continuous process, by land and sea, from any town or village in the world to any other, across many different countries occupied by people of diverse races, colours, tongues, and grades of civilization, are a unique achievement in the history of our age. The railroad, shipping, postal, telegraphic, financial, journalistic apparatus, by which these communications are carried on, constitutes an immense structure of social-economic government. The thought, intelligence, and concordant will required to sustain these communications are already far more than the nucleus of the international mind which it is our object to express in the new forms of political government. The firmly woven bonds of commerce and investment and the tidal flows of labour which, in spite of some obstructions, pulse continually with more power through the world, are constantly engaged in bringing into closer union the arts of industry, the standards of living, the habits, desires, and thoughts of men. The noxious fallacies of an antiquated political economy, which represented nations as hostile beings in commerce as in politics, are rapidly dissolving in the fuller light of international experience. The recent revivals of Protectionism may be regarded as the last death struggle of obscurantist economics enlisted in the ranks of militarism. The formal establishment of international government would be able to appeal to the immense resources of this community of interests and activities which constitutes the economic unity of the modern world. While international finance is the most consciously powerful expression of this unity, organized labour has been long reaching out towards international co-operation, based upon a clearly felt identity of interests and a class sympathy transcending nationalism. Though this internationalism of commerce, finance, and labour proved unable to stem the tide of militarism last year, that is no sufficient reason for disparaging it as a material and spiritual support of the new pacific order. For it has been the absence of any legitimate political organism through which the economic internationalism might operate that has been the cause of its comparative impotence. For, until this political structure has been formed upon a firm basis of international law and representation, the economic spirit of internationalism can exercise no regular or authoritative voice even in those questions of peace and war which are so vital to it. Capital and labour alike are coming to recognize that few of their deeper problems are any longer susceptible of merely national solutions. Markets, rates of interest, wages, and standards of living are more and more regulated by world-forces. The perception of the futility of all attempts either to deny or to reverse these world-forces will more and more lead those who do the thinking for capital and labour to think, not nationally, nor imperially, but in terms of mankind. I have dwelt upon these two modern factors in the world because for a long time they have been straining at the barriers of international politics, endeavouring to get national Governments to patch up little bits of international arrangement by means of particular treaties, conferences, congresses, and Berne bureaux. The era of international congresses, through which we have been passing, has largely concerned itself with trying to create partial and informal substitutes for what should be the work of a co-operative international Government. In view of all these facts, and of the immense extension of world intercourse and sympathy which they attest, how can it be possible dogmatically to deny the feasibility of international government upon the ground that it failed a century ago, and that nothing new of any consequence has happened since to justify a different expectation? What has happened since is the creation and emergence into clear consciousness of an international mind.

CHAPTER XII

DEMOCRACY AND INTERNATIONALISM

THOSE who have regard to what they consider the cold realities of the political situation will probably object that this international mind, if it can be said to exist at all, will not show itself in any Congress of the Powers or in the working of any Council, Concert, or other formally international arrangements which may be the subject of experiment. History teaches us, it will be urged, that every nation always plays for its own hand, is motived by its own essential interests, and will not admit the rightful dominion of any common interest or of any general sense of right as represented in the international mind. This has been so in the past. Alliances, Concerts, and Federations have failed because they were mere balances of short-range interests, the centripetal force being too feeble for any permanent agreement. Must this, however, necessarily hold of the future? I have pressed the argument as to the conscious community of interests which binds together citizens of the world. But it is not necessary to rely upon the utilitarian motive only. Are Justice, Peace, Humanity mere futile abstractions? Will not the palpable Injustice, Unreason, Inhumanity of existing international relations, as dramatized by war, prove powerful pleaders for international thinking? To argue that the international mind, required for the successful working of an international Government, is non-existent and impossible, is to deny that the spirit of education has done anything to broaden the views and to expand the sympathies of men. Now, this is a false account of the moral world of our time. Notwithstanding the hampering traditions of diplomacy, it would be impossible to bring together groups of representatives of the ordinary life of the several nations without discovering in them a capacity for the discussion and settlement of issues by reference to the inherent justice and reason of the case, and apart from any merely national reference. As the immense significance of the work they were called upon to do gripped their minds, it would impress its intrinsic meaning on them and would release them from the bondage of the national standpoint. It would do this by an appeal to the principles of reason and justice within them, which would thus become the moulding influence of an international mind. It is this international mind that has replaced the vague and somewhat sentimental cosmopolitanism which was partly felt, partly affected, by small cultured circles a century ago. It is this new factor in the situation which may serve to falsify the gloomy vaticinations of those who insist that the Utopia of a century ago must be the Utopia of to-morrow. We cannot, of course, assume that this new spirit, and the non-political institutions it has informed, will at once supply the strength and unity of purpose for a stable international Government or even for a simpler League of Peace. But they form a ground of hope.

The measure in which this hope may be realized depends, however, first and chiefly upon the opportunities afforded for this international mind and will to animate and control the political experiments. The type of statesman and diplomatist hitherto responsible for the conduct of international affairs, and the methods of diplomacy employed by them, have been impervious to the healthy penetration of this international mind. Different men, different methods, different motives and ideals are required.

It should be definitely understood that the type of man who has filled our Foreign Office and our Embassies, however "expert" he may have been in the diplomacy of the past, is the reverse of "expert" for the new needs of peace and international government. He must be replaced by men of wider outlook, sympathies, and understanding, who regard themselves as the servants, not the masters, of the nation that employs them, and who will be prepared to conduct the large public business entrusted to them in the open light of day and subject to the same wholesome advice and criticism as is available for the conduct of domestic government. What the open door is for trade the open window is for politics, and a people is wise if it distrusts men who tell them that they can only conduct the public business in the dark. The first requisite of popular control of foreign policy, therefore, is a reasonable publicity. The people must have full opportunity of knowing what is being done, who is doing it, and why it is being done, before it has actually been done. Without this provision there is no safety. For a people to grant an unlimited control of their lives and their money to little knots of unrepresentative supermen, who tell them that the arts they practise are too important and too delicate for disclosure, is a monumental act of folly. But while an informed public opinion is the first requisite of popular control, it must be furnished with the proper instruments and opportunities for acting upon foreign policy. This power it must exercise through its representatives in Parliament. The Foreign Minister must no longer be at liberty to make engagements to foreign nations binding us to future performances involving the vital interests of the country behind the backs and without the assent of Parliament. Ample opportunities must be afforded to Parliament for the discussion of foreign affairs and for receiving information from the Foreign Secretary, and a Standing Committee of Foreign Affairs should be appointed to follow the course of policy more closely than is possible for the House of Commons as a whole.

One other reform is needed to give reality to the popular control, viz. the periodic revision and reaffirmation of treaties and other formal engagements between this and other countries. In this way alone can a full measure of vitality be secured for our engagements and ample opportunity be afforded for effecting such changes as are demanded by the new conditions of the times.

This brief recital of the chief reforms needed

to give validity to popular control[1] assumes, as must be the case, that however large the functions to be exercised by any international Government that may be formed, much would remain with the Foreign Offices and the diplomatic machinery of the several Governments. All matters affecting the relations between two nations, or a small group of nations, would, at any rate in their early stages, continue to be negotiated by the respective national Governments, and only if they reached some sort of strain, or otherwise assumed a position of international interest, would come before the Council of Nations. Moreover, however large the powers of an international Government may eventually become, it is exceedingly unlikely that for some time to come it will be entrusted with any large measure of legislative power. Where legislation is needed to give validity to a decision of the Council, action is likely to be taken by an agreement to promote concurrent legislation in the several national Legislatures. Though the ineffectiveness of such a method will be pretty certain to bring about the requisite enlargement of the international power in course of time, during the experimental period much will depend upon the improved conduct of business by the Foreign Offices and the Diplomatic Services.

But the principles of publicity and popular control, essential for the reform of the national conduct of foreign policy, are not less essential to the success of the new international arrangements.

[1] A fully informed discussion of these reforms will be found in an important little book shortly to be published by Mr. Arthur Ponsonby entitled " Democracy and Diplomacy " (Methuen).

In the selection and appointment of national representatives to the Council, in the discussions of the Council, the sittings of the Arbitration and Conciliation Courts, the decisions and the executive steps to be taken, the fullest measure of publicity is desirable. The notion that privacy and secrecy are conducive to the success of diplomacy is in itself the crowning condemnation of diplomacy. For it is chiefly in so far as diplomacy has been directed to securing private national ends by outwitting or deceiving other States, or to forming special friendships and pursuing the arts of underground intrigue, that the utility or necessity of secrecy is apparent. The defence of secrecy rests on the assumption of the rivalry and antagonism of nations, and the use of cunning to get the better of another nation or to counterwork its plans. The policy of the commonwealth of nations neither requires nor permits such secret arts. The injury they have inflicted in the past is terribly dramatized in the world-war that is waged to-day. For granting everything that may be imputed to the consciously aggressive designs of military and political castes, war could not have been brought about save by playing upon the mutual fears and suspicions of the peoples. No nation could have been made willing to fight but for the conviction that some other nation was plotting to destroy it. This general atmosphere of mistrust and apprehension was the direct product of a diplomacy in which secret treaties, underhand engagements, private conversations, and suspected intrigues were believed to sway the destiny of nations. Every belligerent nation believes that it is fighting a defensive war for its national existence. This false belief is the characteristic and inevitable reaction of secret diplomacy upon the popular mind. The only remedy is to let the peoples know that the business which so vitally concerns them is done openly. The light of day is healing as well as illuminating.

Publicity is the answer to all the trite objections that are brought against the possibility or desirability of democratic control of foreign policy. The people, we are told, are too ignorant to be allowed to take a hand in framing foreign policy. Their aid is only invited for one supreme act of foreign policy—war. When diplomacy has failed, the peoples are called upon to make good the failure with their lives. But if the people are ignorant, to what else is their ignorance due than to the fact that little information and no power of decision were vouchsafed to them? For those who have kept people in ignorance to urge this ignorance as a reason for giving them no power is the most impudent of fallacies. The same answer applies to the frequent taunt that the people are the natural prey of scaremongers and a Jingo press. The agitator and the yellow journalist who work by spreading fears, suspicions, and jealousies, and by imputing false motives to foreigners, owe all their power to this atmosphere of ignorance in which they work.

Again, it is often said that peoples are not more but less peaceable than their Governments, and as testimony we are referred to the wild outbursts of popular fury which some Kruger telegram or some Fashoda incident evokes, and to the enthusiastic rally made by every people to the flag when war has been declared. But neither of these evidences proves the case. There undoubtedly exists a sub-current of pugnacity in every people which, when it is duly stimulated, makes for war. The survival of this instinct will always be a source of danger to the public peace. But it is not self-acting. It responds to the strong stimulus of an irresponsible provocative Press, a Jingo statesman, or the overwhelming appeal of an actual state of war. It responds the more readily and whole-heartedly because it recognizes for itself no real responsibility. A check upon this play of popular war-passion can only come with knowledge and the feeling of responsibility which power brings. This is, of course, the general argument for democracy, as applicable here as in any other department of politics. For the notion that foreign policy is essentially esoteric, and stands apart from all domestic policy, is precisely the falsehood that must be extirpated. It is true that hitherto not only the ordinary citizen but the ordinary Member of Parliament has seldom seriously concerned himself with foreign policy. This was partly, no doubt, because he was conscious of possessing little or no power to determine it, but largely because he acquiesced in the view that foreign policy was a thing apart which might safely be left to those who knew, while he confined himself to matters nearer at hand and more obviously important. No Member of Parliament and no citizen can any longer indulge this dangerous illusion. Every one will see the direct and vital dependence of the internal upon the foreign policy of his country, and will recognize that the only way to retain any real voice in the former is to insist upon a controlling voice in the latter. He will base his demand upon the conviction, not that the public are wiser than their rulers, or as well informed as their expert administrators, but that the policy they will approve will be more consistently pacific. The peoples may not be actively friendly in their relations, so far as they regard one another collectively, but they are not actively hostile. Even the prolonged efforts of a Protectionist compaign, directed to poison the minds of a people against rivals who seek to "steal their markets" and "destroy their trade," does not bring the popular passions near the fighting-point. The active hostilities that endanger peace are mainly attributable, as we have shown, to the pressure of private antagonistic business interests within the State upon the sympathetic personnel of diplomacy. In this pressure we have a rational explanation for what figures on the stage of politics as international rivalry, being, in fact, the rivalry of little groups and interests within each nation "usurping the name and pretext of the commonwealth." The peoples, if the conduct of foreign policy can be put more in their hands, will be more pacific, because in point of fact their interests are not opposed but identical, whereas the opposition of the class interests, liable to control policy under our present secret autocratic rule, is a genuine antagonism certain to breed dissensions between Governments, and always playing into the hands of militarism. The peoples may sometimes be deceived into thinking that their real interests are opposed, but it is more difficult to deceive them (given publicity in the acts of foreign policy) than if the moulding of that policy remains in the power of strongly organized financial or commercial cliques, operating in darkness through their Foreign Offices.

In conclusion, there are two dilatory pleas which deserve attention. The first comes from some who, while professing to be favourable to the general case for popular control, insist that, before any steps are taken to make the control effective, a period of education must intervene. The people must be trained to understand foreign policy before they practise it. They must study the history of foreign countries in their relations to one another and learn something of international commerce and law, and of the racial and other problems which are such disturbing factors in history; they must be acquainted with the procedure of treaties and of arbitration courts, and with other modes of adjusting differences. Now, it must be admitted that a popular instruction upon these lines is essential to intelligent democratic control. But since politics is not only a branch of knowledge but of conduct, it is not possible to postpone the duty of securing to the people self-government in foreign affairs until this serviceable education is complete. For in all conduct, individual or collective, the possession of power and of the responsibility attaching to it is of the essence of the educative process. Paradoxical as it seems, you must do a thing before you can know it. Only by the exercise of self-control can a person or a people learn the art of government. Only in that way can it gain a full incentive to acquire the special information and capacity of judgment which the educationists are anxious to impart. The process of exercising power before the mind is properly informed is indeed a risky one, but these risks and the mistakes which they involve are not peculiar to foreign policy. They belong to every art whatsoever, and condition the experiment of life itself. Moreover, there are two considerations which mitigate the danger lest an ignorant mob-mind should drag a nation into ruin. If it is not true that knowledge is power, it is true that knowledge is indispensable to the direction of power. An ignorant mob-mind will be distracted, and will seldom possess the unity of self-confidence requisite for the strong pursuance of desperate causes. No ignorant people could commit the criminal conduct imputed to Germany. Again, some self-preservative instinct may not unreasonably be ascribed to a people. If it be premised that no real clash of interests exists between the nations, and that one nation does not stand to gain by another's damage, but that, on the contrary, peace and co-operation are obviously profitable to both nations alike, this fundamental mutuality will, quite apart from an intellectual comprehension of its workings, insensibly operate upon the general mind and will to keep nations in the path of sanity. No such instinct is available to keep in peaceful courses a diplomacy whose secrecy is so well adapted to the conflicting pressures of rival business groups and military castes within the several nations. An opponent of popular control would need considerable hardihood to maintain that self-government in foreign policy could lead to worse disasters than the method hitherto in vogue.

The second dilatory plea urges the impossibility or the undesirability of one nation practising publicity and popular control until all others attain the same level of enlightened policy. This view rests on the assumption that the nation which shows its hand will be at a disadvantage, which assumption in its turn harks back to the notion that nations in their dealings with one another are competitors, not co-operators. But granting that there will always continue to be a place for bargaining, in order that one nation may get its proper share in some common good, such publicity as we desiderate need not and would not impair this process. Publicity and popular control do not imply that every tentative step taken, every communication made, should be an immediate subject of debate in Parliament or in the country. What is demanded is something very different—viz. that sort of real control exercised by the directorate of a business company over their managers and agents, to whom they entrust the detailed conduct of negotiations along lines which they have sanctioned, though all binding agreements and contracts must be submitted to them for their assent. It is the main course of policy that must be kept continuously before the public eye, and it is the determinant acts of that policy which must receive the direct sanction, beforehand, of the representatives of the people. There is no reason whatever to assume that a State which so conducts its foreign affairs will be placed at any disadvantage in dealing with other States whose ways may be less liberal, or that negotiations cannot pass between two States behaving so differently towards their peoples. The power of the American Senate and its Foreign Affairs Committee, and the publicity attending its procedure, are nowise shown to be detrimental to the conduct of foreign affairs in that country. The fact that a Foreign Minister cannot bind his country to an important undertaking, without obtaining the open and express assent of its representatives, does not, as is sometimes suggested, involve a weakening of foreign policy. It is not a really strong foreign policy where a Minister, acting entirely on his own initiative, is able to make engagements involving his countrymen in obligations which he does not know they will be willing to accept when the time comes for meeting them. Publicity is a source of strength, not of weakness, for sound foreign policy, and its adoption and practice by a few genuinely liberal nations would do more than anything else to liberalize the methods in the more backward States. More than any other course of conduct it would make for that education of the mutual confidence of nations which is the indispensable condition of secure international arrangements.

It is to publicity, the regular reliable formation and co-operation of public opinion among the different peoples, that we must look for the prime support of peaceful international relations. No mere structure of treaties, Councils, Courts, or other instruments of international Government will be of real avail for the maintenance of peace and the promotion of active co-operation among nations, unless in all or most countries this informed and active public opinion exists. It may not always find full and formal expression through parliamentary or other representative institutions. If we were to insist that no safe or sane relations could be formed between any nations whose Governments were not developed along lines of formal democracy, the outlook would indeed be dark. But important as is popular control through Parliament, publicity and informed national opinion are more important. For in the critical events of history no Government, however autocratic, can effectively ignore, defy, or antagonize the general sentiment of the people. Once secure that the course of international relations is conducted openly, and that organs of public opinion are no longer able to poison public opinion at the source, by spreading false suspicions and sowing fears and animosities, the first moral condition of sound internationalism will have been attained. Publicity is more than half democracy in the conduct of foreign policy. Upon this "open door" for news, ideas, and feelings, the education of the national mind, we shall rely for the building up of that larger moral organism which is to function in politics, the international mind.

* * * * *

At the end of this war, although the different peoples may still dispute the rights and wrongs of its immediate causes, they will seek its deeper origins in the belated survival of the evil arts of militarism and diplomacy, with their false outlooks and their group pressures. They will refuse to allow the practitioners of these arts to resume their sway over their lives and to force them once again like dumb, driven cattle towards the slaughter-house. They will insist that the obsolete rhetoric of Power and Sovereignty, with the ideas of exclusiveness and antagonism which it sustains, shall be swept away, and that the affairs which concern nations shall be set upon the same footing of decent, reasonable settlement that prevails in every other human relation. They will require their statesmen and their representatives to think out and establish the necessary arrangements for doing this. When they perceive that these arrangements, to be effective, involve an International Government, with council, courts, and an executive strong enough to carry into effect the common will of nations, they will not be deterred from pressing to this goal by theories about the absolutism of States or the biological necessity of war, or by false analogies from history, but will definitely declare for a Commonwealth of Nations as the only security for peaceful civilization in the future.

INDEX

UNWIN BROTHERS, LIMITED, THE GRESHAM PRESS, WOKING AND LONDON